YOUR NEXT
BOLD
MOVE
for Women

9 Proven Steps to
Everything You Ever Wanted

by Wendy Capland

Published in the United States by Vision Quest Consulting

www.visionquestconsulting.com

ISBN-13: 978-0-9859762-1-7

DEDICATION

To my girlfriends and sisters of my heart.

To my parents who have always inspired and motivated me
to reach for the stars.

To my children who bring my life so much joy.

And to my husband, who still makes my knees weak.
I love YOU more!

Table of Contents

Introduction

I turned 50 and my world turned inside out. Why could I not feel satisfied? I was lucky my outside circumstances were all fine, but on the inside I felt like a big mess. I was uncomfortable with so many parts of my life that just yesterday seemed to be working smoothly. I knew there was something inside of me waiting to be born; yet I couldn't quite grasp it. My voice was changing, and it was unfamiliar and creating quite a mess as I tried to speak about the things I wanted. My wants and needs were shifting, and I couldn't understand why these feelings were so strong all of a sudden and why they were creating havoc in my seemingly happy predictable life. Everything about me felt uncomfortable, and I did not understand what was happening. Everything on one level seemed fine, but fine was no longer enough. I wanted more. I yearned for more. I craved a life where I could find myself—be born anew somehow—but I didn't even really know what that meant. It was all so confusing.

Then I began the journey toward loving myself and learning to see myself in all my glory. Learning to see myself as the world saw me—in my better moments, of course.

Sometimes I wonder, what if the woman I am meant to become is already there inside of me, and I don't have to behave like someone else to "get there"? What if the woman I am meant to be has been there all along, just waiting for me to see her? What if the woman I am meant to become is already me and I am already her, and somehow I have yet to discover and fully embrace her? What if it isn't all that hard to find her and let her spread her glorious wings, and I just haven't known how to do it?

Why Are We Not Enough?

Why are we so hard on ourselves so much of the time? So many of us have a little voice in our heads whispering that we are not good enough, not smart enough, not thin enough, tall enough, rich enough, sexy enough…blah, blah, blah. Do you know the voice I'm talking about? I wonder, why it is so hard to quiet that voice enough to hear another voice—one that speaks to us of self-mastery and supports our feeling good about who we are?

Of course, we can blame the media for flaunting its ridiculous anorexic models and suggesting that we look and dress a certain way, or the advertisers for selling the promise of a better-looking, younger "me" if only we would buy their products, or the corporate board rooms and executive suites that insinuate we are not good enough to have an equal seat at the table. There are so many things in our culture that contribute to our lack of a sense of self. And yet, all of these dynamics collectively feed into our own uncomfortable belief that somehow we are not enough just as we are.

I wonder, do I really want to become someone else or have a different kind of life? Or do I just decide I must be insufficient in some way when I compare my own circumstances to someone else's? I have to admit there are days I dream of what it would be like to be Lady Gaga, Princess Kate Middleton or as she is more formally known, Her Royal Highness Princess William of Wales, or Oprah, or have the easy life my neighbor seems to have. But deep, deep, deep down inside, I have a feeling that being Lady Gaga, Princess Kate, Oprah, or even Susan down the street isn't all it's cracked up to be. And in my more quiet moments, I really love the woman I am. Honestly, I would rather be a better me, if I could just figure out who that might be.

The "If I only was different" syndrome is not healthy for us. It undermines our spirits and sabotages our efforts to express the gifts and talents we already possess. More importantly, it interferes with the process of becoming who we are meant to be. Not loving our true selves diminishes our light. We lose our sparkle and when that happens, and we begin to feel smaller than we actually are. Why would we choose to do this to ourselves if we could avoid it? Who wants to be small? No one.

Who would choose to feel crummy about herself? No one. We don't like walking around feeling "less than," but most of us do just that, and do it way too much of the time.

This book is for women who want to find themselves and discover their hidden gifts and talents, and bring them to light to share with the world. It will give you a step-by-step process to listen to your inner guide and move into action with more joy and purpose. I guarantee it will give you some peace within yourself and quiet the little voice in your head that tells you that you are not enough. It doesn't mean you don't need to lose that extra weight, and it doesn't mean you shouldn't stop eating all that junk. It doesn't mean you won't need to make some changes in your life that you know only you can make. It *does* mean that it's time to choose to live into your full power, to find your true voice and use it to its fullest expression—to discover yourself anew.

What are you waiting for? The time is now!

At the Sacred Edge

Midlife is a sacred time in a woman's life. It is often a time of great change for men and women alike. But for women, it's a time when we start to yearn and long for something in a way we have never experienced before. Maybe we are sick and tired of listening to the negative voice in our heads tell us we are not good enough, and we're tired of feeling dissatisfied with ourselves and our lives. Maybe we care a little less about what we are not and more about who we are becoming. Maybe we are finding respite from the onslaught of hormones that have been raging wildly through our bodies, and we finally have some inner peace (well, at least some of the time). Before midlife arrives we "want" certain things, but this midlife longing feels different. It is a new, deeper kind of yearning toward something we can barely articulate, and yet we feel its power surging through us and calling us forward.

For most women, this "blessed unrest," as I like to call it, is a time of personal discovery we have been waiting for since the day we were born. Introducing itself to us sometime in our late 40s or early 50s, it can often remain with us into our 60s, depending on when we finally start to act on it. Blessed unrest is a personal invitation to each of us to come into our fullest blossom, as the Universe quietly whispers to us and nudges us toward what's next. I've heard it said that the two most important days in our life are the day we are born and the day we discover *why* we were born.

Even though this time of personal discovery into the woman we are meant to become is one we have been waiting for since the day we were born, most of us don't hear this initial gentle calling toward her—or if we do, we don't know what to do about it. Because we have been so busy being busy all our lives, we often aren't familiar with listening to our inner voice—the voice through which the Universe speaks to us. So the Universe keeps whispering, and we keep doing what we have always done: going to work, managing our households, hanging out with our friends.

But because the Universe is always conspiring on our behalf, the voice inside of us becomes louder and louder until we can no longer ignore it, and something inside of us starts to yell, "Help! Something's not right here! I don't feel like myself!" Even though we still don't know what the heck is happening to our busy but predictable lives, we suddenly find ourselves wondering if it's time to quit our jobs and try a new career; if it's time to stop tolerating our husbands and leave them; or if it's finally time to try to find out who we really are underneath it all.

At this point we feel like we are in a big crisis, which of course we are—a crisis of self. Now we have no choice but to finally stop and listen: really listen for what's next for us. This yearning to hear the deep calling is so profound that we can no longer ignore it. And part of that longing is the wish to know how to really listen and how to sort through what to do with what we hear.

The good news is that this is a time of great and exciting renewal in a woman's life. The bad news is that this midlife exploration can be difficult, and many of us can feel like a train wreck as we are trying to navigate our way through it. You know it's happening to you when you start to feel out of sorts, unsettled, edgy, and itching for something you can barely describe; but if you don't do something about it, you are going to explode.

Fifty and Not So Fabulous

Right around the time I turned 50, somewhere in the Universe someone thought it would be a good time to flip a switch and have me reexamine everything in my life: my health, my marriage, my work. One day I went from being happy and more-or-less satisfied to craving something I could not quite put my finger on. And even though I had no idea what was happening, I knew I could not ignore it. I was unhappy, restless, crabby, and sick with ailments that seemed to come out of nowhere. I broke out in hives, and no doctor or dermatologist (and I saw many) could identify why I had them or where they came from. Not just a few bumps; I was covered all over my arms and legs for more than six months. And boy, was I itchy! And miserable. And then one day without any warning, the hives mysteriously disappeared. My doctor could not explain it and neither could I. But in some deep place within myself, it did not escape my notice that my itching on the inside for something more in my life showed up as itching on the outside, too. Like the skin I had had for all these years somehow didn't fit me anymore. Maybe if I had listened to my inner itching sooner, I would not have gotten hives. Who knows? It was part of my crisis of self.

And then there was the acid reflux. Or at least that's what it felt like and what the doctor called it, but no gastric medicine, either over-the-counter or prescription, could touch it. I had every test known to gastronomical woman done, but there was no known cause for my intense discomfort. But when I started exploring my life purpose, aligning the things I really cared about with my work and reexamining how I spent my time, well...the discomfort in my gut stopped. Okay, so it took three years for it to completely disappear, but no treatment or medical intervention helped until I started to seriously reevaluate my life. My condition, where I literally had trouble swallowing, actually made perfect sense, as I was no longer able to swallow the way I was running my life. Only then did I realize that if I didn't figure out how to approach my life in a new way, I was going to be in one medical crisis after another, and they were probably going to get more serious. I decided that listening to my soul calling me forward was much more enjoyable—even while confusing at times—than being incapacitated or debilitated. Thus, my journey had begun. I started to discover what I cared about, who I was as a person and as a woman, and what I wanted to do with the gifts and talents I already knew I possessed.

Come Out, Come Out, Wherever You Are

Why wouldn't you want to create a future you will adore and turn into the woman you are meant to become? On one hand, you can barely imagine what I'm talking about, and on the other, in a quiet, deep place within yourself, you know exactly what I'm saying, and it's as if these words were written just for you. Which, of course, they are—calling you forth into your own spectacular, powerful, wondrous, beyond-imagination, beyond-belief self to utilize all your gifts and talents. To spread your wings, because that's what wings are meant for.

This journey requires quiet and the courage to look at what you want, as well as a bucketful of support. You cannot do it alone. It requires the holding, nurturing, and witnessing of community. It requires one step at a time to create a life you fall in love with.

No woman escapes untouched by this process. So many of us recognize that we are at the edge of manifesting and expressing our full potential and power. Join the millions of women who are starting to hear and feel the woman inside who is just waiting to burst through. We don't need to be someone else. We are not *meant* to be someone else. We need to find the magnificent, beautiful, powerful woman we already are, and bring her forth with her own unique voice. We need to awaken our potential. Women, at this time in our lives, we are standing on the edge of our own evolution, of our own transformation. This is the perfect time to kick it into high gear. What else do you have to do?

Don't you hear the little voice inside of you whispering your name, calling you to come out into life, into your future? You know, the voice inside of you that's been busy running your life, busy raising a family, busy building a career—busy being busy. Until now.

But now it is time.

"Hello there, sweet one," it says. "It is time. It is time to use that beautiful voice that has been waiting for just this moment in your life to come forward."

Our inner light...why is it so hard to let it shine brightly? What are we afraid of? Are we afraid of what our voice might sound like or say if we actually spoke what our heart desires? Why does it scare us to imagine ourselves living fully into the woman we are meant to become? What's so dangerous about being bold, speaking our truth, and shining brightly?

It is time.

I am, we are, calling you forward into the woman you must learn to love more than anyone—into yourself. Into your future. Come and have a peek at your true self. Know that the world is meant to have your unique gifts and talents, your inner sparkle and magic, and the touch that is uniquely yours. There comes a time in every woman's life where it is time to bring herself forth in ways that she has never dared before. And the world is ready. Trust that it is your time. If not now, when?

And So It Begins

So here we are, dear one, at one of the biggest crossroads in your life. The woman you are meant to become is waiting for you with open arms, calling you forward to embrace her. It takes courage to leave the road you've been traveling and choose this path. It's unfamiliar and unknown. And yet somehow, as unfamiliar as it is, something deep inside knows that it feels like coming home.

Standing at the crossroads, you have arrived at a time of your life where you hear "the call," even if you are not certain exactly what it is saying and what you are meant to do. And amid all the uncertainty, you feel the anticipation and the glorious excitement when you answer the invitation to meet yourself anew, coming face to face with the woman you were always meant to become.

When I was at the height of uncertainty in my own turmoil and chaos, at my own crossroads, I did what most women do when they feel confused and a bit crazy—I called my girlfriends to talk it through. Thank goodness for girlfriends, right? They hold our hand as we share parts of our lives that feel hopeless. They help calm us down as they hear us talk about our heart's desires. They make us feel better as they listen deeply without trying to fix or change us. They "get us" at our core. They know what matters. Girlfriends are a lifeline to help us see a brighter day when we've lost sight of it ourselves. Even though they often don't *do* anything but say, "Oh honey, I'm so sorry, this must be so hard for you," or "Yes, that's it! Go for it!," they make all the difference in our world.

I don't even want to think about what my life would be like without my girlfriends. They walk next to me as I go through the big challenges in my own life, and I walk with them, too. When I was sorting through crises in my marriage, they were there, holding my hand. When I was feeling lost and bereft when my children left and went off to college, they promised me I would survive and even learn to enjoy this new chapter in my life. When I was sorting through which road to take in my career, they listened deeply and offered to help me, over and over and time and again. When I had one crazy medical diagnosis after the other, they counseled me to look deeper into my heart to hear what it was crying out for. And when I was faced with a breast cancer diagnosis, they all rallied to reassure and comfort me. My lifeline, in times of crisis, and of course in times of joy, is my dear, sweet girlfriends.

The midlife crisis of self, where we reexamine who we are and where we are going, is one of those times we need girlfriend handholding. It's one of those times when we need constant reminders that we have what it takes. We need extra reassurance that we have the support to step into the unknown and into our future. We have our girlfriends to make the journey easier. We support each other and remind each other that we are truly loved for who we really are at our core.

So, girlfriend, let's walk together. You and me, right now. Girlfriend helping girlfriend. Let's discover the road ahead, waiting just for you. As women, it is not our way to make this journey alone. You are not *meant* to do this alone. Now is the time. Don't you think you've waited long enough?

Here I am, ready to walk with you, and I'm up for taking the journey together! Your new voice and power await you. Let's figure out, with a sprinkling of girlfriend magic, where you are headed next, what your next move might be, and how you might get there. I promise that when you arrive at your own front door, you will be greeted by the arms of your beloved—you!

Let's Talk

Let's start our girlfriend journey by getting a hot cup of tea and sitting down together for a nice chat. (No, really—feel free to stop reading now, and go get a cup of coffee or tea before you read on!) Last weekend, my neighbor asked me if I would like to have tea on Sunday afternoon because she needed a girlfriend to talk to. We spent a wonderful few hours together listing all the things that were making us crazy in our lives, ranging from our spouses to the work scene. We explored them from all angles, laughing and holding each other's pain in a sacred, confidential place in our hearts. It was great therapy for us both, and when it was over we were able to go back to our lives with our hearts a little lighter and our spirits a little brighter.

So, let's imagine we are drinking tea together, just the two of us, and you tell me what's not working in your life right now. Really, stop right now and make a list—a long list if you have one. Lay it on me and don't hold back! This list will provide you with clues for the road you are meant to follow. Trust me, you have nothing to lose except a little list-making time.

This process of kvetching (Yiddish for complaining or whining) will actually help you decide what things are really important and need your attention. It's a great way of getting it out of your system and freeing yourself up. I guarantee you will feel enormously better afterward. Go get a piece of paper or grab your journal and make a list of everything that is making you crazy, miserable, and out of sorts.

You might be thinking that it's against the rules of etiquette to fully and unabashedly express your unhappiness and dissatisfaction. Too bad, right? Yes, because it feels so good to just let it rip. And it's good for our health mentally, physically, and spiritually to let the craziness we feel escape our bodies in order to shift our perspective.

I sometimes say to a client who is struggling with a difficult issue, "Take a few minutes and list all the stuff about this situation that's making you crazy so you can feel better. Then let's see if there's anything you want to do about it." I strongly suggest making a list anytime you are in crisis, and especially when you are at a crossroads. It's a remarkably productive exercise. And by doing it you will see, maybe for the first time, a new possibility or a new way to move forward. Having a new perspective provides a spark of light that begins ever so slowly, or even suddenly in some cases, to lift great burdens off your shoulders. I guarantee it.

Here we go. Choose the items from the list below that are not working well in your life right now and write them down. It's not an exhaustive list, so feel free to add more of your own! And don't feel you need to kvetch about everything on the list, either. If something is working just fine, celebrate it versus kvetching. Then, taking one item at a time, write down your reasons why this is so. What is not working? Why? What part of it is making you unhappy? Why are you feeling conflicted? Describe the conflict, as you see it, as honestly as you can. Pretend you are telling a girlfriend what's not working in your life. Take some time and kvetch away with me, your new best girlfriend!

Family
Career/Work
Finances/Money
Home
Health
Friends
Relationships
Fun
Community
Spirituality
Confidence/Self-doubt
Personal Development
Professional Development

You might be wondering, okay, so now what? You have this big mess of a list and you are either feeling better than ever as you anticipate heading toward your next move, or worse than ever as you look at it and wonder how the heck you got here in the first place. I believe acknowledging and facing our current circumstances head on, for better or for worse, is a powerful first step in moving toward having the lives we want to live and becoming the women we are meant to become.

Now, let's take your list and choose one area to work on first. Which one should you choose? Maybe the one that makes you the most sad or seems the most challenging or is your highest priority. Or maybe the one that isn't the most emotionally difficult but that you have the energy to tackle. It's up to you. Whichever area you pick, you must be committed to making a positive shift and a bold move in this one area of your life. It may be tempting to choose more than one, but my recommendation is to work on one at a time, and when you've succeeded with the first area, you can go back to your list and select another one.

I'm going to introduce you to my **9 Steps**, the ones I have used for many years that you can use, too. You can use my **9 Steps** to resolve your toughest issues and take action, moving yourself forward one step at a time. Now that you've chosen a topic, let's get started!

Chapter 1

Check Your Inner State

Do you sometimes feel like you are on the edge of something wonderful in your life that you can't quite put your finger on? Do you sometimes feel a voice starting to bubble up inside of you, if you could only find a way to give power to it? Do you sometimes wonder, who is this woman inside of you that's been waiting and waiting to come forward? Don't you want to finally meet her?

Of course you do. Come on. Let's walk this road of discovery together. The good news is the answers are inside of you (yes, it's true, they are!) and all you need to do to begin is a little internal excavating.

The call forward into what's next in our life comes from listening to the guidance of our inner voice. Our inner voice is like a GPS, mapping and navigating the course toward our next soul-purpose destination. This journey can be unsettling, especially in midlife, where we have spent years being sure about what we want, but all of a sudden, somehow, we aren't so sure anymore. This unsureness has us start questioning and reexamining everything in our lives. We wonder if our marriage still fits us. We question whether we want to stay on the same career path. We notice that half our life is over, and we start to think that if we are really going to make any kind of footprint or leave any kind of legacy, maybe we should ramp it up. But how?

During this time of reexamination we often feel confused and sometimes cranky, but we don't know exactly why or exactly what to do about it. The ability to listen to our inner voice and check in with how we are feeling is a valuable tool that we must learn to use in navigating these roadblocks in order to move forward successfully. And, might I add, to move forward with less chaos, fewer crises, and fewer health challenges, which seem to be my modus operandi.

Before my hives and gastro problems showed up, I noticed all sorts of clues as to why I was out of sorts that I ignored. At the time I didn't realize they were signals to pay attention to, and I had no idea that by ignoring them they would find new ways of getting my attention that were unpleasant, to say the least.

During this time of unrest, I wrote the following in my personal journal, which tells me I did start to notice my inner state and how I was feeling.

> *I'm nudgy. I'm antsy. I feel unsettled. Inside my body I feel like I'm pacing back and forth, back and forth, waiting for whatever is supposed to happen next.*

> *I'm the type of person who usually knows what she wants and knows how to put a plan together to get it. It's one of my strengths. I'm pretty good at it. It's been working for me. But for some reason, this linear process is not working for me anymore. Why?*

> *Here's how it used to work. It's really quite simple. I set a goal. I set action steps to get to the goal. I track my progress, make adjustments as needed, and keep right on going until I achieve my goal and get whatever it is I want. I am driven, determined, and persistent when it comes to meeting personal or professional goals I set for myself. In fact, I'm a bit relentless until I get what I want. Not in a bad way, but in a "stay focused on the goal, keep your eye on the prize" way. I pretty much always know where I am in the process and what I need to do to get to the finish line. Life has worked smoothly this way for me for so many years.*

But, like I said, it isn't working any more. No matter how hard I try to figure it out, I have no answer that seems right. I don't know why I'm feeling unsettled, I just feel of out of sync somehow and I want something that I can't quite put my finger on. It's not that I am unhappy with my work or that my personal life isn't fine...I don't know...

So I am trying to be patient. And not whine too much. I am trying to stay open to whatever shows up. I am having conversations with colleagues and friends that might help me unfold the mystery. So I wait. And I write. And I know that whatever is next is right around the corner for me to discover. And I hope it happens soon because I'm driving myself crazy!

Ask yourself right now: How has my life been feeling to me lately? Is there something bubbling up inside of me? How would I describe *that* feeling? Sometimes this feeling can be experienced as general malaise or boredom, or as a yearning for something more, new, or different. Only when we are able to identify the discomfort can we do something about it. The idea is to pinpoint exactly THE THING that is making you crazy and allow yourself to fully experience the discomfort you are feeling. No more denying it, avoiding it, or pushing it away. If we are willing to listen and use what we hear, feeling uncomfortable can provide us with the opportunity to learn and explore what's working in our life, and what is not.

Getting Started

The best way to start figuring out what's calling you forward is to start noticing what's bubbling up inside of you and to raise your awareness about what that is. It doesn't matter whether you are someone who is certain about a specific idea or project you want to put boldly into action, or someone who has no idea what it could be. Maybe it's the thing you've been dreaming about, but maybe it's just something you haven't gotten to and are ready to start. Either way, the place to begin is to check your inner state.

What is an inner state? An inner state is how you feel inside. Happy. Satisfied. Blissful. Cranky. Out of sorts.

Complete this sentence with a word or phrase that will help you describe your inner state: I feel _____ about my life right now.

Checking in with your feelings is more commonly associated with using your heart to inform your decisions versus using your head. Feelings may or may not make sense at first.   Feelings are not logical, but they are like soul signposts, guiding us in the perfect direction for our next move. As I said earlier, my outer world seemed just fine, and logically everything was groovy, but on the inside, my heart was crying out for something I could not quite put my finger on.

My dear friend Kate Harper says, "An inner restlessness is often the spark of creativity." Creativity boosts can sometimes feel very uncomfortable, but more often than not, they give me an answer or a direction I would never have discovered otherwise. In my experience, change can feel uncomfortable simply because it is unfamiliar, not because it's not good for you.

Begin the journey of awakening your inner goddess by identifying an area of your life where you feel dissatisfied, unsettled, or frustrated. To do this, ask yourself: What part of my life isn't working all that well? What part of my life is out of alignment and needs some tweaking? I know this may sound like a counterintuitive or negative way to approach creating the future, but I have found that specifically identifying the source of my discontent is often the first clue that helps me move forward. Where are you now feeling a bit out of sorts or even really dissatisfied? (You may use the one you discovered through the exercise in the "Let's Talk" section; just pick one for now to work on.)

The area of my life that I want to be different is

_____.

Some people know exactly what needs to change in their lives and how to do it. Most of us at midlife, however, don't know what we want now. I know I didn't. For many of us, the inner journey to discovering ourselves anew begins with awakening to the woman we have been waiting our whole lives to be. Who wouldn't want to meet her? Imagine, just imagine for a moment, that she is already there inside of you and you just have to find her. And what if it is easier than you thought? Awesome thought, right?

So let's start the process of birthing this new fabulous woman inside of you!

In the section below, there are some resources to help you with your first step: *Check Your Inner State.* Complete the suggested exercises and use the additional resources to help you move forward.

Exercises and Activities

This exercise is a closer look at how you are feeling about the area of your life where you are dissatisfied.

- Journal about your inner state, the area in your life where you identified feeling restless and unsettled, and also about the category or area that is not going all that well right now. If you have more than one area or are not sure where to start, make a list and then pick one to journal about and work through the **9 Steps**. Treat this exercise like an inquiry into what you're feeling and what that might reveal to you. You will have more fun and be more successful at doing this if you approach this exercise with curiosity and a playful mind versus being oh-so-serious. Ask yourself, "What's this about?" Engage in it as an exploration, like a treasure hunt, seeing what you can uncover. Find out new information about yourself as you explore what your heart is revealing to you.

- Journal about the area you have selected each day for about a week. You can journal longer or shorter periods of time each day depending on what you uncover and how much you feel like writing. Many people ask, "How long do I need to journal?" I'm not such a consistent journal writer myself, but my recommendation is for a minimum of 10 minutes or for as long as you need to feel satisfied. The purpose of journaling is to help you clarify the core issue that you're investigating.

Brainstormers to Check Your Inner State

1. Inner Inquiry
   a. Notice if you're restless, out of sorts, and/or not quite yourself.
   b. Feeling nudgy is a signal—what's your best guess as to what is going on with you?
   c. Are you crabby, unsettled, bored, and/or dissatisfied in any particular area?
   d. Do you feel in a kind of crisis?
   e. Inquire, wonder, and be curious about what it could be, who it is related to, or why you are feeling this way.
   f. Ask yourself *where* you feel restless—in your work, your relationships, your home, your body, and/or your spirit?
2. Do you love what you're doing and the people you're working with?
3. Have you lost touch with what you're doing and why?
4. Are you asking yourself, "Is this all there is?"
5. Are you wondering what you are meant to do, or what is the legacy or contribution you want to make?

6. Are you tired—physically, emotionally, spiritually—and feeling like you're not sure you "have it in you" anymore?
7. Are you tired of being tired?
8. Are you willing to learn to live with the discomfort as you sort through what you really feel?

Summary

The first step toward making your next bold move is to awaken the powerful woman sleeping inside of you. Find her voice. Learn what she has to say that will help guide you forward. You are meant to travel this path toward her but you must learn how to listen deeply, to hear her call and the messages she has for you that are meant for you to follow. We await your discovery with great anticipation. For you are meant to come forth in all your glory. And the world is waiting. It's not complicated; just practice how to listen, my darling. Listen to that inner voice that guides you forward.

And by the way, it can be fun and liberating when you finally put your finger on what's going on, what you want, and where you are headed. And your heart and soul will sing with the sheer joy of your discovery. Come. We are here to help each other awaken into our best selves. If not now, when?

The next step in creating what's next for you is to *Give Yourself a Time-Out*, which we will discuss in the next chapter. We all need to rest. Most of us are overwhelmed, over-committed, and over-stressed by the way we run our lives and move through our days. We need to create time and space for reflection to give ourselves "white space" to just *be* with ourselves. In *The Writing Life*, Annie Dillard writes, "How we spend our days is, of course, how we spend our lives." In these quiet moments, as we experience the lessening of pressure and the absence of stress, we are able to feel and to hear the next right thing to do, the next step we are meant to take.

Stay tuned for Chapter 2, *Give Yourself a Time-Out*!

Additional Resources

Here is a list of things that I read, listen to, and watch to help me identify and deal with my inner state being out of sorts, unsettled, and unsure of what I want next.

Books:

> *Eat, Pray, Love* by Elizabeth Gilbert

> *Mists of Avalon* by Marion Zimmer Bradley

> *Many Lives, Many Masters: The True Story of a Prominent Psychiatrist, His Young Patient, and the Past-Life Therapy That Changed Both Their Lives* by Brian L. Weiss

Videos:

> **The Shift**
> Awakening our connection to something larger than ourselves.
> www.theshiftmovie.com

> **Randy Pausch Last Lecture: Achieving Your Childhood Dreams**
> www.youtube.com/watch?v=ji5_MqicxSo

Music:

> **"Total Praise"** by Richard Smallwood

> **"Celebrate Me Home"** by Kenny Loggins

> **"On Holy Ground"** by Barbra Streisand

Free downloads:

Oprah's Soul Series
Listen to audio clips related to specific topics.
www.oprah.com/oprahradio/About-Oprahs-Soul-Series-Webcast

Women on the Edge of Evolution
Free teleseries with 21 of the world's leading female spiritual luminaries, thinkers, artists, and agents of change in an unprecedented conversation.
www.womenontheedgeofevolution.com

Chapter 2

Give Yourself a Time-Out

When I was a little girl and had done something naughty, my
mother would send me to my room to reflect on the seriousness
of my transgression. I spent a lot of time in my room having what
my mother called "time-outs." It's hard to know if I was really all
that mischievous as a child or just stupid enough to get caught.
Time-outs in my house felt endless to me, and I often wished my
mother would have yelled at me instead so I could get back to
playing and having fun instead of "thinking about what I'd done"
for what seemed like hours, alone in my room.

Early in the punishment phase I felt righteous, angry, and certain
that whatever I had done was definitely not my fault. I hated
being banished from the world, uncertain of how long I would be
imprisoned in my room. Once I got over the "being angry" stage,
and realized I wasn't going anywhere fast, I settled into a
delicious reverie of imaginary play and dream time and began to
create a world around me that made me feel better. I often put
classical music on my record player, which I also liked to listen
to at night before going to sleep. I would take out drawing paper
and crayons and doodle the time away. Sometimes I wrote
stories and acted out plays with my dolls. In a strange way, being
by myself for a while left me feeling calm, settled into an
alternate reality, and enjoying a place where I could shut out the
rest of the world and just *be*. My mother was probably hoping I
was spending my time-out feeling sorry for whatever I had done,
but as I grew accustomed to the quiet, I was happy just being
with myself.

As an adult, I think a time-out or time spent alone is a marvelous
thing. It gives us a chance to quiet our minds so we can settle
down within ourselves and connect to what's most important to
us. This feminine style and approach invites us to be quiet and
slow down versus moving into action too soon. The New England

culture in which I live currently is based heavily on the puritan work ethic: work hard, get things done, and don't waste time with any nonproductive activities. This masculine approach can be exhausting. Without the balance of the feminine it creates many negative results in our lives, some of which include higher levels of stress, poor health, and a loss of purpose and passion for the things that really matter to us. It's actually a gift to rest and replenish ourselves. Doreen Virtue, a Ph.D. and a fourth-generation metaphysician, says, "We sometimes accomplish more by taking a break and daydreaming about possibilities, which are intuitive guidance about our next step." As I'm writing this, I hear the 60s song, "Feelin' Groovy" by Simon and Garfunkel playing in my head: "Slow down, you move too fast. You got to make the morning last...."

We all need to rest. Most of us are overwhelmed, over-committed, and over-stressed by the way we run our lives and move through our days. We all need quiet and slow moments in order to experience the absence of pressure, and to simply reduce the effects of everyday stress. We also need time and space for reflection and to give ourselves "white space" to just be with ourselves. My dear friend Melanie says, "It's important to slow down to give ourselves space to hear what God has in mind for us."

We all need to take a break from doing and even *thinking* about doing. We need respite from our perpetual thinking in order to hear, feel, sense, and *know* what's really meant for us to do next, and what steps we need to take to get there. It feels so delicious to have the time to rest and replenish our bodies, minds, and spirits, especially when we give ourselves permission to do so.

Making your next bold move is fueled and guided by on-going time-outs, which is another good reason to find a way to schedule them into your life.

Everyone disengages differently. What may be relaxing for me might leave you feeling agitated, and what may be revitalizing for someone else might leave you feeling drained. Each of us must find her own way to replenish herself and step out of the day-to-day rollercoaster.

I'm not really the laid-back, relaxing type of person, so time-outs are really important for me. Being a bit tightly wound, and having days over-scheduled with all that needs to get done, it takes a lot for me to relax; I mean *really* relax. So I have to practice the art of relaxing. I have many different time-out strategies and I alternate between them depending on the day and my mood. Sometimes I even do more than one at a time often determined by either how bad my day has been or how stressful I think it might become. My favorite thing to do to rest and replenish myself is to sleep. I love my bed and my soft feather pillows, and there are days I wish I could stay in my bed forever. Sometimes I climb into bed as early as 9 o'clock at night and journal or read. I then sink into a long, luxurious night of sleep and dream, not waking until 7 or 8 o'clock the next morning. For me, this is the ultimate in restfulness.

This past summer I took four weeks off from my crazy work life and rented a house on a lake in New England. Hearing the water lapping on the shore outside my bedroom window, I slept like a baby night after night, knowing it wasn't my own home with a million things needing to be done the next day. It was the perfect time-out. Among the other things I did to rest and relax were going on long morning walks, dozing in the lounge chair by the water, and reading for hours and hours at a stretch. I feel grateful to have been able to take so much time away from both my work and my day-to-day personal life. My husband was a saint as he managed his work and life around my need for rest. It felt like a luxury for me to meet this need so fully.

You may not be able to take a month away like I did, but you could sleep, nap, meditate, walk in the woods, sit by the ocean, or go on a personal retreat. Anything that takes you away—alone— from your work and your family is helpful, even if it is for an hour, a day, or a weekend. It can be a small, daily strategy or a single, big event. You might have to experiment a bit to find the approach that gives you a deep inner sense of rest, replenishment, and rejuvenation.

Taking Guilt-free Time-outs

Taking a time-out without feeling guilty is really important and may take some practice. Most of us feel so guilty about giving ourselves the gift of rest that it becomes more stressful to rest than it is to keep going at our breakneck pace. You might be saying:

> "I could never leave my family; I would feel too guilty."
> "I don't deserve it."
> "I can't do this, it takes too much time; I have no time."
> "When I have free time I would want to be with my family."
> "I could never do something without my family."
> "I have things to do, I have responsibilities. How could I take the time?"
> "What would my family or others think of me?"
> "I feel like I would be cheating or getting away with something."

Many of us have self-defeating thoughts that talk us out of caring for ourselves. I have them, too. When I am feeling strong and have a deep knowing that I must take a time-out, I say to my inner critic, "Thanks for sharing," and then I go forward and make my plans. In moments when I am feeling overtired and less than powerful, many things happen, none of which are pretty. I feel depressed. I complain a lot. Sometimes I get sick. And inside, I feel like a miserable wreck and hate being with myself. During these times, if I wait for the negative self-talk to completely disappear or even subside, I will most likely never take the time-out I really need to shift my mood and create a life I love. Whenever I feel crabby, stepping back and taking some time alone helps me see things in a new light. The short- term benefit is that I am almost immediately less cranky, and there are long-term benefits as well.

Good Reasons for Giving Yourself a Time-out

There are many benefits to taking a time-out. Overall, time-outs take us out of the day-to-day and give us access to a clarity and perspective we don't normally have. Given the time and space to see things in a new light, we can often solve problems or challenges we have been facing for weeks, or even longer, by simply taking a step back. Time-outs are the perfect opportunity to be curious about our lives and wonder how we might move forward with something we haven't had the time to fully think about. Time-outs are crucial for being able to plan and dream about our next bold move and to birth something new in our lives.

Time-outs play a critical role in impeccable self-care—the one essential thing that guards our good health and makes it possible to receive all these benefits. Our body needs to be cared for, and without giving it the time it needs to recover from the craziness of life, it's just a matter of time before our health will be affected negatively. We can take care of everyone else and neglect ourselves for only so long. When our health is impacted negatively we are the ones who suffer the most; but when we suffer, the people around us suffer, too. We're stressed out and out of sorts, or we're sick and not much fun to be around.

So time-outs have direct benefits for our loved ones as well as for ourselves. These benefits include having a healthy body and a grateful spirit, feeling happy, playful, and joyful, and being more relaxed. In my house we have an expression, "When Mom's happy, everyone is happy." And I know one of the keys to my own happiness is having time to myself. I like to think about it this way: when I take care of myself, I'm giving a gift to myself *and* to my family.

My mother no longer banishes me to my room and I no longer play with dolls, but I find incorporating time-outs into my life today just as wonderful for my creativity and my sanity as they were many years ago. My four weeks at the lake, resting and walking, is where I came up with the idea to write this book. My month alone in Florida during one cold New England February saved me from doing something stupid to my marriage. When I had the opportunity to focus on what I loved most about my husband versus giving all my attention to every little thing that drove me crazy, I remembered how much I adored him. My walk on the beach one summer Sunday afternoon gave me an insight that helped a client be promoted to the next level in her job. And my many Sunday mornings when I just lounge around in my bed with a good book, a hot cup of tea, and my fluffy pillows recharges my batteries to face another week.

Getting Started

So now what? How do you get started? There is no better time than now to start incorporating time-outs into your life. I look at it like practice. If you are like many of us, you may not have had much practice at this new behavior. Don't worry if you don't get it right. There really *is* no right, so feel free to experiment until you notice that you feel good. Give yourself time to find out what works for *you*. Try stepping away from your busy life for an hour, an afternoon, a day, or even a few weeks. You'll know you are getting the hang of it when your whole being, heart and soul, feels luscious and satisfied and you cannot imagine life without your own special brand of time-outs.

Exercises and Activities

Write your answers in the spaces provided below.

- I currently take time-outs for myself in the following ways that I really love:

- I like doing the things I listed above because... (Write as many reasons as you can think of.)

- What other ideas do I have or would I like to consider for taking time-outs? (Consider big ones *and* little ones.)

- Have a conversation with a friend, mentor, or coach and share the following thoughts:

  1. Recently, I have felt an inner restlessness (refer to Chapter 1) about:

  2. In the past, one thing I have done to take a time-out is to:

  3. In the future, I would like to add to my life the following ways to take time-outs:

- Being accountable to someone other than yourself can produce powerful results. Have a conversation with a friend, mentor, or coach and share the following commitments:

  1. I am committed to setting aside _____ hours/minutes for myself _____time(s) a day/week/month to _____.

  2. I will experiment with a practice of _____ as a new time-out behavior for _____ days/weeks/months.

Brainstormers to Give Yourself a Time-Out

1. Rest, replenish, regroup, reprioritize.
2. Sleep, nap, meditate, journal, read.
3. Walk in the woods, bike, swim.
4. Go on retreat, take time away.
5. Step away from your computer (work).
6. Step away from your role (family).
7. Be by yourself *without* guilt. Create a "no guilt allowed" zone for yourself!
8. Give the gift of time to yourself so you can give more fully to others.
9. Plan time away or plan a stay-cation so you can schedule time for yourself.
10. Build up your reserves—we all need to refill our cup.
11. Get quiet and enter a contemplative state where you can hear your own truth.
12. Use your time-outs as a space to be creative and create.
13. Incubate. Gestate with yourself.
14. Stay light with your certainties.
15. Be curious about your life. Wonder...

Summary

Making a bold move requires both inner quiet and outward action. The second step toward making your next bold move is to take a time-out, to put yourself in a state of relaxation and rest, to experience the absence of pressure and daily stress, and to hear your own inner voice guiding you to what's next.

Taking time-outs requires practice to integrate them successfully into your daily life. Have patience with yourself as you experiment, explore, and enjoy restoring your body, mind and spirit. With practice, you will put yourself in a state of inner relaxation and be better able to hear your heart's desires, messages, and guidance. You will learn to listen deeply for your next steps on the journey toward your next bold move. What is your inner voice trying to tell you?

The third step in creating your next bold move is to *Listen UP! to Your Intuition.* Your intuition can give you answers to some of your most pressing questions and information about which direction to choose when making your next bold move.

Stay tuned for Chapter 3, *Listen UP! to Your Intuition.*

Additional Resources

Here is a list of things that I read, listen to, or watch to help inspire me to take a time-out.

Books:

> ***Infinite Possibilities: The Art of Living Your Dreams*** by Mike Dooley

Videos:

> **Create Abundance Affirmations**
> http://www.youtube.com/watch?v=GSpITM08X3I
>
> **The Power of Time Off** by Stefan Sagmeister
> http://www.ted.com/talks/stefan_sagmeister_the_power_of_time_off.html
>
> **Kuroshio Sea**
> Second largest aquarium tank in the world—a peaceful and restorative video.
> **http://www.youtube.com/watch?v=u7deClndzQw**

Music:

> **"If I Were Brave"** by Jana Stanfield
>
> **"Strength, Courage & Wisdom"** by India Arie
>
> **"Tomorrow (A Better You, Better Me)"** by Quincy Jones

Chapter 3

Listen UP! to Your Intuition

According to Dictionary.com, intuition is referred to as "the direct perception of truth or fact, independent of any reasoning process." Intuition is a way of knowing something based on instinctive feeling rather than previous or conscious cognition. This chapter is focused on learning how to increase our ability to access our instinctive feelings so we can use our intuition to guide us to our next bold move.

We all have our own inner guidance system, although we use it to various degrees in our daily lives. My intuition has often come in handy to warn me of some impending danger, point me in a new direction, or delight me with an unusual coincidence or synchronicity. I, like many of you, experience my intuition as an inner voice, or sometimes, a gut sense. On a good day, I believe I am getting better and better at listening to my intuition. On a not-so-good day, I'm oblivious to anything but my to-do list.

Although I had known about intuition for many years, I had always felt as if others had a better connection to theirs than I did to mine. One night, however, I got a taste of what my intuition could do for me. It was the first time I clearly remember following my instincts instead of wasting time arguing with the voice in my head and thinking that I was only imagining things.

I was driving home late at night after eating dinner out with a girlfriend. It was raining so hard that I could barely see through my windshield, even with my wipers on the fastest setting. My visibility was so awful that I considered pulling over under a bridge on the highway until the rain had a chance to let up. As I got ready to pull my car over, I got an indescribable, creepy feeling and started thinking, "It's probably not a good idea to pull over this late at night. You're all alone, what are you thinking? Something about this doesn't feel safe." And then, for some inexplicable reason I started to repeat out loud, over and over again, "Dear God, help me get home safely." None of this "crazy" thinking seemed rational at the time. I thought I was just freaked out about the rain and how hard it was to see. I felt the need to pull over because the road was almost invisible in the rainstorm, but for some reason, at the same time I felt like it might not be the safest thing to do. I kept driving and was relieved to finally reach home, a bit frazzled but safe.

Here's the kicker. The next morning as I was getting ready for work, I was listening to the television news. The newscaster reported that the previous evening, at the precise time and exact location of the same underpass where I was contemplating resting, a gunman was shooting a rifle randomly into oncoming traffic. Needless to say, I was so stunned I could hardly speak. In that moment I realized that my intuition may very well have saved my life that night. I will forever remember that May evening as my intuition wake-up call. And I have come to understand that in most cases, if we can quiet down and really listen, our intuition has messages that are meant to help guide us, whether they save our life or just point us in a direction we are meant to go.

I am certain that my intuition gives me more messages than I am able to hear or notice, especially when I am so busy with my life that I don't build in the time to quiet down and really listen. After that evening in May, I started to read books and take some classes to help build what I like to call my "intuition muscle." My spiritual teacher, Greta, says, "There are many ways to access our intuition. Most of us have a mode that is uniquely ours and works for us more effectively than the other methods. Some people's intuition speaks to them through images, others feel and sense things, and some people actually hear an inner voice that gives them instructions to follow." Every one of us has intuition, where our internal voice gives life to our inner knowing, and has an inner guidance system that gives life to and cultivates our intuition.

I'm one of those people who access my intuition through seeing images. It's a little hard to explain. It's not that I actually see something solid by using my eyes, but I get a flash of a picture in my mind. It pops in and then disappears just as quickly, with some sort of message attached to it. Here is an example: Once, when interviewing a young woman for a receptionist job in my department, I had a flash that I should hire her. I saw for a split second that if I hired her, it would be short term, as I would be promoting her into a professional level job quickly—although this first job would be a great stepping-stone for her career. I did hire her, and sure enough, within a year she was promoted to administrative assistant and then to recruiter in the Human Resources department.

What Does Intuition Have to Do with Making Your Next Bold Move?

Our internal voice has intuitive messages to help guide us toward our next bold move as well as the step-by-step processes necessary to turn our ideas into reality. If we are too "busy being busy," we cannot access our intuition and hear our inner guidance. This is one reason why it is so important to give ourselves the time-outs I discussed in Chapter 2. Using our intuition allows us to open our hearts to hear—and suspend judgment about what we hear—in order to uncover our own deep knowing. It's a state of openness. What do you need to do to hear yourself more clearly?

In 2006, my intuition was really kicked up and running full throttle as I was lying on my friend Melanie's table having a Reiki session. Before starting, she asked me to set an intention for the session. Since I had been struggling and *really* wanted to know what my life's purpose was about, I decided to go for what I thought was the impossible. I set an intention to know with certainty what I was put on this Earth to do. While half asleep and totally relaxed, hoping for some answers, I suddenly had this strong unexplainable thought (of course because my intuition works visually, this thought showed up like a movie picture playing in my mind) that I had invited a group of women into my living room and we were sitting around drinking tea and eating chocolate while talking about the things that mattered most in our lives. While I was confused as to what these women had to do with my life's purpose, a little mermaid spirit guide showed up in the dream and answered, "We have showed you this picture so many times before; you can continue to ignore us or you can just get started." Still unsure what this all meant, I woke up and told Melanie about the mermaid and her message. Then I slowly started to remember way, way back in my memory bank that I had dreamt many times about my living room and women. And although I still hadn't a clue what the heck this had to do with life's purpose, I followed my intuition blindly and called up ten women, inviting them over for tea, chocolate, and conversation.

Well, that was over 700 women ago, and now we have a thriving organization of women supporting women to make their next bold move. (You might want to come to one of our retreats. Find us at this link: http://visionquestconsulting.com/events/.) That the idea to build a community of women was born out of intuition is deeply satisfying to me on a personal level. It allows me to do some incredible personal transformation work with incredible women.

Intuition has been referred to as the language of the soul. The author of *Conversations with God*, Neale Donald Walsh, says, "Listen to what you are feeling. Feelings reside in the soul, and the soul is God-in-you. In this place is your truth, and it is in no other." The territory of intuition can be compared to the ocean—vast and mysterious. As we begin to swim around and immerse ourselves in this unknown territory, we start to notice what stirs, inspires, and informs us. We begin to see and feel more clearly what's next for us in our lives, even if we don't quite understand what it all means, just like my dream during my Reiki session.

The Masculine and the Feminine

Accessing your intuition is a feminine approach to problem solving and to creating what's next. The feminine gets internally and externally quiet in order to hear our inner guidance when it speaks. The feminine takes time out in order to allow creative ideas to come forward. The Herman Group, a collection of consultants, futurists, and speakers who stay on top of global trends, reports fascinating results of IBM's last Global CEO Study. According to the 1,541 CEOs, general managers, and senior public sector leaders who were polled from around the world, creativity was the number-one leadership competency for organizations in the future. These organizations encourage top talent practices by supporting experimentation and innovation throughout their companies.

I'll be curious to see how this actually works in practice, as I have a hard time imagining any boss saying, "Take time out to rest and replenish yourself so you can be more innovative and creative. In fact, don't even come into work for a few weeks so you can dramatically increase your chances of hearing your inner guidance on this issue." Ha! I do believe this competency is critical for future leadership, though. It will challenge the deeply held belief that working long hours without taking vacation time is necessary to climb the ladder of organizational success.

What I do know is that by allowing ourselves the gift of seemingly "doing nothing," we can hear our inner guidance directing our next move. In contrast, our masculine aspect often gets frustrated and thinks time is a-wastin' if there are no meetings, nothing is scheduled, the computer is off, and, instead, a good walk in the woods is the primary activity planned for the day.

The feminine style connects to intuition as an inner exploration of what's most important and what it means in the scheme of things. The masculine style, by contrast, uses the mind versus intuition to analyze its way out of any given situation. The

feminine, by leading with intuition in this step, allows the heart
to lead, whereas the masculine is more inclined to let the head
take the reins. Although analysis and logic play an important
part in choosing what to do next, I am suggesting that you begin
by asking your heart what it wants, and practice leading with the
feminine approach.

Getting Started

Learning to *Listen UP! to Your Intuition* awakens your inner
desires. And yes, the best way to get started is by practicing. It's
more fun and less stressful if you don't put pressure on yourself
to do it perfectly. Practice is just experimenting and trying
something out, over and over again, without the expectation that
it should be successful. It's just practice. One thing I love to do is
to look for patterns and clues and treat them like I am on a
treasure hunt to discover something new and interesting.

You can start by becoming aware of what is happening within
you and around you. Start noticing synchronicities, coincidences
or connections that occur in your life in interesting,
unpredictable ways. A few years after starting my women's
organization, a women's university contacted me to develop a
partnership where my firm provided leadership coaching at its
annual leadership conference. I'm not sure that would have
happened without a combination of my corporate management
consulting work *and* my work with women. It has made me
wonder whether there is more to this life-purpose, working-
with-women thing that has become a solid thread of connections
and synchronicities over the past couple of years.

Remember that there are many different means to accessing
your intuition—hearing, seeing, and feeling/sensing. Wonder. Be
curious. Start with a single idea or a hunch. Let yourself wonder
or be curious about an idea or a hunch you might have. Notice
the "aha moments" or inklings that come to you. What idea keeps
floating through your mind, or before your eyes, or speaking to
your gut over and over again?

You don't have to have all the answers or be certain about anything. I'm rarely certain about anything my intuition guides me to do, but I follow it anyway, thinking there must be some reason I have this hunch. Just start noticing what catches your attention. You might have a few false starts. That's okay. Give yourself permission to experiment. It can be fun to inhabit parts of yourself that have been vacant or unexplored, and it's a wonderful experience to develop a quiet relationship with yourself. Let the creative force of the Universe flow through you to help you clarify the impulses behind your thoughts.

Experiment. Test. Evaluate. Testing and evaluating the results of your intuition are important steps, so that you know whether you are on track or not. The simplest way to do this is to start a log or journal where you write down your intuitive hunches and then rate their validity. Ask yourself, "Did it come true?" If you had a deadline or timeline associated with your hunch, was that accurate as well? If not, what were your results, and what was the gap between your hunch and the result you obtained? This written log will help you see patterns as to how your intuition works. Some people have good intuition, but the timeline is a bit off. Others are more accurate when it comes to certain people, events, or situations. The only way you will know what is true for you is by keeping a log for a while so you can test and evaluate the results you get.

A fun and simple thing to do is to practice naming who is calling you on the phone before you answer it or check caller ID. Again, start to log your results so you are accurate in your assessment as to how you are doing. I don't think I've ever had much fun practicing a skill as I have with practicing and developing my intuition!

Exercises and Activities

Write your answers in the spaces provided below.

- When or where does my intuition speak the loudest to me? (Examples: Walking in the woods, taking a shower, driving my car, listening to music.)
  I get my best insights when I am

  _____.

- What is my primary mode to *Listen UP! to My Intuition*? (Hear? See? Feel?)
  My primary mode is _____.

- Have you noticed anything unusual happening to you lately? Do you have a sense that the Universe is trying to tell you something? If so, write about it here. If you can't think of anything specific, make a wild guess and see what you discover. Remember, there is no right or wrong answer, just whatever occurs to you in this moment. The objective here is to notice and experience the world around you giving you clues and hints as to what is next for you.

- What recurring thoughts or persistent ideas have you been having? Are they connected or related to anything in particular? Consider the possibility that your intuition is speaking to you.

Brainstormers to Listen UP! to Your Intuition

1. It's hard to hear your intuition when you're busy, busy, busy.
2. Cultivate the ability to listen to your inner voice.
3. Notice where the synchronicities occur and where patterns reveal themselves.
4. Allowing your intuition to guide you gives life to your inner desires. What stirs your soul?
5. Intuition means you don't have to already know or be clear about anything. Just listen with your heart.

Summary

Making your next bold moves requires you to consistently tune into your intuition to guide you in the right direction. Making a bold move requires quietness in order to hear what your intuition is guiding you toward next. Intuition and inner guidance is as powerful a tool as learning how to execute and put into action your goals and plans. This book gives you the inner tools to make your next bold move in the first three chapters. As we move toward Chapter 4, we start to make the transition to outward action and execution.

To see if you are on track with your own internal guidance system, ask yourself if you feel certain within yourself, if you have a feeling that you are headed in the right direction, or if you can recognize that you are experiencing a sense of joy. If not, you need to change course. Albert Einstein, winner of the Nobel Prize in Physics, whose theory of relativity revolutionized our understanding of matter, space, and time, said, "The only real valuable thing is intuition. There is no logical way to the discovery of these elemental laws. There is only the way of intuition, which is helped by a feeling for the order lying behind the appearance."

Check Your Inner State, Give Yourself a Time-Out, and *Listen UP! to Your Intuition,* the first three steps, are meant to work together synergistically to help you gain clarity and move toward what's next for you. Successfully listening to and letting yourself be guided by your intuition in your daily life requires practice. Have patience with yourself. With consistent practice, you will find that you can easily put yourself into a state of inner relaxation and be better able to hear your heart's desires, messages, and intuitive guidance. The practice of accessing your intuition will help you learn to listen for and trust your next steps on the journey toward your next bold move.

The fourth step in creating your next bold move is to *Prepare for the Game.* Developing and nurturing our bodies, minds, and spirits are critical to successfully navigating the leading edge of our potential. Imagine what would be possible if we played, experimented, and practiced stretching ourselves just beyond what we thought might be possible or realistic. What if we broke through our own self-imposed limitations? There is a goldmine of potential for each of us to mine. How exciting is this?!

Stay tuned for Chapter 4, *Prepare for the Game.*

Additional Resources

Here is a list of things that I read, listen to, or watch to inspire me to *Listen UP! to my Intuition.*

Books:

> *Awakening Intuition: Using Your Mind-Body Network for Insight and Healing* by Mona Lisa Schulz
>
> *Divine Intuition* by Lynn A. Robinson
>
> *Compass of the Soul: 52 Ways Intuition Can Guide You to the Life of Your Dreams* by Lynn A. Robinson
>
> *101 Ways to Jump-Start Your Intuition* by John Holland
>
> *Conversations with God* by Neale Donald Walsh

Videos:

> **Jill Bolte Taylor's Stroke of Insight**
> http://www.ted.com/talks/lang/eng/jill_bolte_taylor_s_powerful_stroke_of_insight.html
>
> **PS22 Chorus Sings "Landslide" by Fleetwood Mac**
> http://www.youtube.com/watch?v=f2p5augniQA
>
> **Elizabeth Gilbert: A New Way to Think About Creativity** http://www.youtube.com/watch?v=86x-u-tz0MA

Music:

> **"Something Good"** by Juan Luis Guerra
>
> **"Adi Shakti"** by Mantra Girl

Chapter 4

Prepare for the Game

Making a bold move takes persistence, commitment, focus, and faith in order to pull it off. Making your bold move can be fun and easy, but sometimes it's just plain hard work. You have to be in top form physically, mentally, and spiritually to move toward what you want and to play what I like to call "the bold move game." Developing a three-pronged approach to preparing yourself for the game is our focus in this chapter, giving you tools to help you become more effective, efficient, and self-confident.

Preparing yourself for your next bold move is similar to how Olympic athletes ready themselves for competition. Olympic athletes take their training seriously. They develop their physical, emotional, and spiritual fitness with equal intensity. That's what I'm asking you to do—develop your body, mind, and spirit so you can be in top form. This may seem extreme, but I believe that preparing for the game requires extreme measures if you are going to be successful. There are no shortcuts here. It takes hard work and dedication. And for myself, I find that the personal rewards make it worth it, even though there are days when I fantasize about just staying in bed.

On the day of the big game or event, an athlete will spend many hours getting him- or herself ready before even stepping onto the field to compete. According to sport psychologist Shane Murphy in "What it Takes to be an Olympic Athlete,"

> Consistent mental training is as much a key to success as is great physical preparation.....What's fascinating is that we find that athletes often don't need to be perfect to succeed. Being in the "zone" isn't about perfection as much as it is about staying in the moment, not worrying about failure, and not worrying about what the result

might be. I find every athlete to be unique in their approach to that "zone," but they use some combination of psychological skills such as visualization, goal-setting, concentration, relaxation or mindfulness, psyching up, positive self-talk and developing a consistent routine in order to get there. Once they're ready, they focus and let it happen. Their bodies are prepared to succeed—usually it's the mind that can get in the way—if you let it.

Making *your* next bold move requires that you take the time to prepare and seriously care for your body, mind, and spirit with that same level of intensity.

In previous chapters, we focused on the feminine approaches of self-reflection and inner inquiry. In this chapter we begin to move into action; therefore the masculine style predominates and is most often required.

Many people start their day by stumbling out of bed and inhaling a cup or two of coffee. Most of us do very little to prepare ourselves for the day ahead before launching into it or starting work, even if it's a day when we have a big event happening. We are so busy running around trying to get everything done that we rarely take the time to prepare ourselves to play the game we're playing—a game that starts each and every day. As the day progresses, many of us have increased levels of stress and anxiety that reach critical levels, and we never get the chance to stop and catch our breath before it ends with our falling exhaustedly into bed. When we don't stop, breathe, and check in, we tend to spend our days just trying to catch up. When your mind and body are in a state of perpetual stress, it's almost impossible to acknowledge and listen to your intuition (the feminine approach) or be in top form to execute your next bold move (the masculine approach).

Not so long ago my early mornings were full of stress. Even before I got out of bed, I would lean over and grab my cell phone to see if I had any texts, read my emails, notice whose turn it was to make a move on the multiple mobile-app games I played, and finally check my Facebook page to see who was doing what. When all that was done, I turned on my laptop to double check my email to make sure I didn't miss anything from the time I checked the messages on my cell. I would do all of this before even getting out of bed, saying good morning to my family, or brushing my teeth. Not a powerful way to start my day, to say the least. Oh my goodness, I'm exhausted and embarrassed just writing about it!

I now reflect on this crazy habitual morning routine with a sense of disbelief at the insanity of how I chose to start my day. At the time I didn't see anything wrong with it, but one day on vacation, having broken the routine because I didn't have cell phone access, I realized I wanted something more for myself. As you read about my old routine, I'm sure some of you are recognizing yourselves and saying, "That's me!" Luckily for me and before it was too late, I realized this crazy routine of prioritizing and responding to everyone besides my family wasn't working for me, and I made a dramatic change. I now begin and create my day from a more centered and connected place, which has reduced my stress levels, increased my creative thinking, and given me time to think about my top priorities for the day.

Now I wake up earlier and start six or seven days a week with exercise and a morning smoothie. If you knew my past, you would know what a big deal this is. I feel stronger and more physically fit at 50 than I did at 20, and my body thanks me for it! Once a month I get a massage to support my body exercising hard every day without getting hurt. With my new routine, I haven't had a stiff back or achy body part for many years now, and I'm certain it's because I am taking impeccable care of my body.

We all know what we need to do to prepare our bodies: eat well, exercise regularly, and get enough sleep. Nutritionally it's simple, although not always so easy to do. If you get off track, just start over again. Get focused on and committed to your physical health by getting rid of processed sugar in your diet, reducing caffeine and carbohydrates, and eating in a balanced, healthy way with a focus on organic fruits, vegetables, grains, protein, and fats. The key is both exercising and eating well consistently, not just thinking about it. What are you doing to take impeccable care of your body? What more could you do?

To develop and prepare my mind, I am a voracious reader of the topics that relate to my current next bold move. This includes research on the Internet as well as reading professional journals, articles, and books. I also attend two to three conferences in my field each year to trigger new thoughts and ideas for my business, my life, and where I'm headed next. I get a sense of energy and excitement when I am working on and reading about my next bold move topic, because I have extreme passion for it, and so will you. Immersing ourselves in our passions is really effortless and fun and rarely feels like hard work.

Preparing your body and your mind are mostly masculine-centric activities, as they require a plan, goals, focus, drive, and consistent action to exercise and eat nutritiously. The masculine side of us must get in gear to get in action. Eating well and exercising require action. In contrast, the feminine side requires self-reflection, which is helpful in developing our spirit.

To develop and prepare my spirit requires me to be quieter, exploring how I think and feel, which therefore makes it a more feminine approach where I am focused on the inner and not the outer. I'm not really the religious type, so I don't find my connection to spirit by attending church or temple. Instead, my spiritual training and development comes from my attending a yearly psychic development course and a monthly Mystery School program with a shaman, who helps me connect to my spirit and quiet my mind and body so I can hear what my spirit wants to say. I could really do more in the spiritual development arena, as I tend to lead with my masculine side and move into action a little too quickly. I've learned that being too busy and not slowing or quieting myself down puts me out of balance. It's important for those of us who move through the world by doing, doing, and more doing to bring more of the feminine into balance within ourselves.

What can you do to develop your body, mind, and spirit so that you are ready to play the type of game you are meant to play in the world?

You don't have to do the things I do, but you do need a consistent body, mind, and spirit development plan that works for you so that you, too, are in top form to play your game. Yes, it takes hard work. It takes dedication to something bigger for yourself, something that you really want, something deep in your soul. Bigger, so when the usual sabotaging self-talk starts to surface that sounds like: *"I don't have the time. It's too hard. I'll get to it later. I don't know how I could possibly fit it in. I'll just take a day off today. Oh, it's just a few cookies,"* you can be bigger and bolder than your negative self-talk. In addition, when the going gets really tough, you have the strength to hang in there and not give up.

It's easy to give up when things seem hard. Don't do it. Hang in there. It will be worth it in the end. Last month, I started a new exercise routine to shape and sculpt my abs, arms, and legs. For the first two days, I thought I would collapse from the rigorousness of it. It was really hard, but I didn't give up, even though I wanted to. Really, really wanted to. I thought the instructor on the DVD was crazy—there was absolutely no way I could do what she was doing. As the days went by, it didn't get easier. It was still really, really hard. But much to my utter surprise, I can now do all the exercises! I'm more used to the rigor and some how I am still going strong. And I'm really proud of myself for kicking up my exercise routine a notch and showing up each morning to try another day on the mat with this crazy chick of an instructor who makes it look ridiculously easy. One day at a time, one leg lift at a time.

If we don't take charge of our lives in all the areas of body, mind, and spirit, we will often start our days with a weight on our shoulders and with our minds already in gear. What you want is to powerfully create your day, powerfully create your next bold move, and powerfully and with self-confidence do the things that bring you joy, even when life throws you challenges.

Astronaut Edgar Mitchell, as he was returning from outer space, described the moment he saw the Earth as an experience that radically altered his worldview. Gazing out the window of the spaceship, he remarked, "The real frontier is not outer space but inner space." Within two years of his expedition, Edgar Mitchell founded the Institute of Noetic Sciences, a nonprofit membership organization that conducts and sponsors leading-edge research into the potentials and powers of consciousness. The Institute is dedicated to expanding science beyond conventional paradigms.

Preparing your body, mind, and spirit by doing your own practices in each of the three areas will give you access to the leading edge of *your* potential. And who knows where it will lead you—just as Edgar Mitchell could have never predicted he would found an institute. Your dedication to your daily, weekly, and monthly practices will set in place a foundation that will allow you to live your life so that you flourish into your greatest capacities. Wow, who wouldn't want that?!

Getting Started

If you are inspired to start big and bold, go for it. When I decided to exercise seriously, I went all out and decided to do it every single day. But if the task ahead feels daunting, starting yourself off with baby steps is far better than not taking any steps at all. If this sounds like you, and you would rather start slowly, then begin where you can and build yourself up. Just start.

Begin by asking yourself some targeted questions:

- What kinds of things could I incorporate on a consistent basis to enhance the health of my body?
  Ideas and examples: Join a gym, hire a personal trainer, dance, hike, ski, walk, jog, eat well, see a nutritionist, do a food cleanse.

- What kinds of things could I do to enhance my learning in the area of my next bold move? Pick an area you want to learn more about.
  Ideas and examples: Read, start or join a mastermind group (a peer group whose members are dedicated to helping each other reach their professional goals), attend a professional conference, get certified in an area of interest, talk to people who are doing what you are thinking about doing and ask them what they like and don't like about it.

- What spiritual practices or rituals would serve me best at this time? What would allow me to cultivate a quiet mind and give me some personal reflection? What would I do to feel more balanced, confident, grounded, and calm?
  Ideas and examples: Work with daily affirmations, journal, walk in the woods alone, go on retreat, meditate, garden, paint, sing, get an energy medicine treatment such as Reiki or craniosacral therapy, get a tarot card or psychic reading, talk to your spirit guides, go to church, talk to God.

Have regular daily practices so you can learn to cultivate different ways of connecting with yourself.

In his book *Mastery*, author George Leonard says, "To practice regularly, even when you seem to be getting nowhere, might at first seem onerous. But the day eventually comes when practicing becomes a treasured part of your life. Ultimately, practice *is* the path of mastery. If you stay on it long enough, you'll find it to be a vivid place, with its ups and downs, its challenges and comforts, its surprises, disappointments, and unconditional joys." The purpose of having practices is to become clearer about what's most important to you, to reveal unseen blind spots, and to unwind assumptions about the way things are that aren't nurturing us.

What constitutes "practice" is unique to each person, and ranges from ancient wisdom traditions to self-created practices. Whatever you choose as your practices, shape and craft them so they contain the following elements:

> **Intention** – Decide what you want and ask for it or declare it. An example of this would be a New Year's resolution: I intend to increase my health through exercise and eating well.
>
> **Attention** – Shift where you place your attention. Refine it to shape and shift your views and beliefs. These practices will remind you where you are going, give you the energy to get there, and keep you sane and de-stressed.
>
> **Repetition** – Reprogram your actions and behaviors with repetition.
>
> **Guidance** – Get help and guidance from a coach, trainer, advisor, or mentor.
>
> **Community** – Do your practices in community and not just alone, as community is a powerful and effective way to keep yourself on track and feel supported.

It's great when you can design practices where you are totally absorbed—where you lose track of time *and* feel nurtured. Don't forget the hard things like my exercise routine: the things that aren't always easy but are well worth it. At the end of the DVD I do feel nurtured, and I often look at myself smugly in the mirror and say, "Wendy, you rock! Good job, girlfriend!"

Exercises and Activities

- What are the fundamentals, consistently practiced; in the areas of body, mind, and spirit that will give you balance in your life? Make a list.

- What is the one thing, if you started to do it now, would have the most impact and influence in your life?

Brainstormers to Prepare for the Game

1. Ready yourself for your next bold move. Treat it like you are entering an Olympic event.
2. Train. Meditate. Stretch. Visualize. Journal.
3. Eat well.
4. Prepare for your day. Don't start in reactive mode.
5. Develop daily practices. Develop good practices. Have discipline and rigor.
6. You can't expect to be in top form if you don't prepare to be.
7. It takes something to make a bold move. It's not for sissies.
8. Do real exercise.
9. What are the fundamentals, if consistently practiced, that would give you joy, energy, and prepare you for your game?

Summary

Whatever you practice you will get good at. If you practice complaining, you will get good at complaining. If you practice feeling like you have no control over getting what you really want, you will get good at that, too. Ask yourself, "What am I practicing?" Then design daily practices that inspire you and support you and the health of your body, mind, and spirit.

I hope you're getting the message here. If you start off every day in a prepared, positive frame of mind, you will be connected to your inner guidance before the *external* gets ahold of you. Make necessary shifts in any bad morning habits you have as you create a new routine that nurtures and prepares you for your game. The question is: Will you give yourself the opportunity? The choice is always yours. You'll feel like a new and improved version of yourself if you take action to prepare yourself. Put into practice the things that will serve your highest good, and keep yourself aligned and on track to your next bold move.

Like an Olympic athlete, you too must be in shape—body, mind, and spirit. Don't wait. Shake up your life in a good way and get started now! I promise you'll love it no matter how wide the gap between where you are and what you think will serve you best.

The fifth step in creating your next bold move is to *Get Clear About What You Want.* Getting crystal clear about what you really want to create will dramatically increase your chances of achieving it.

Stay tuned for Chapter 5, *Get Clear About What You Want.*

Additional Resources

Here is a list of things that I read, listen to, or watch to help inspire me to *Prepare for the Game.*

Books:

> ***Tracy Anderson's 30-Day Method: The Weight-Loss Kick-Start that Makes Perfection Possible*** by Tracy Anderson

> ***Younger Next Year: Live Strong, Fit, and Sexy—Until You're 80 and Beyond*** by Chris Crowley and Henry S. Lodge

Animal Speak: The Spiritual & Magical Powers of Creatures Great & Small by Ted Andrews

A New Earth: Awakening to Your Life's Purpose by Eckhart Tolle

Crossing the Unknown Sea: Work as a Pilgrimage of Identity by David Whyte

The Schwarzbein Principle: The Truth About Losing Weight, Being Healthy, and Feeling Younger by Diana Schwarzbein and Nancy Deville

Mastery: The Keys to Success and Long-term Fulfillment by George Leonard

Videos:

Jessica's Daily Affirmation
http://www.youtube.com/watch?v=qR3rK0kZFkg

Music:

"Baby I'm a Star" by Prince

"Eyes on the Prize" by Mavis Staples

"Conviction of the Heart" by Kenny Loggins

Chapter 5

ut What You Want

I think most of us don't really know what matters most to us deep down inside. It's not that we don't have things we care about or that we aren't able to say what those are. What's missing is the answer to the question, "For the sake of what?" Reverend Martin Luther King Jr. said, *"Our lives begin to end the day we become silent about things that matter."*

Why do you care about your health, or your family, or being a good provider? What's the primary reason for your caring? Why do these things matter to you?

To increase your chances of successfully executing your next bold move, it must be closely tied to what you really care about—something you *really* want. In order to turn any idea into reality, we must be clear about exactly what it is and then determine, in fact, that we really do want it. Let's explore this idea of how we decide what we want from many different angles, in order to help spark your own inspiration and to manifest your desire into reality.

Want, desire, and need usually precede the appearance of an idea. I believe spending time clarifying what we desire will increase our chances of getting it. Sounds like this should be pretty simple, doesn't it? My personal experience, however, has shown me it is not as easy as it sounds. Here is why. We care about a lot of things. We might want a lot of things, but which are the right ones to act on? Which is the bold move we want to put into play?

Then there is the other side of the coin: What about those of us who are crystal clear about what we want but have not yet gotten there? Why is that? Like my friend Paula, who is crystal clear she wants and needs a job, but she has gone months without one. In Paula's case, she remains uncertain about her next career move, and that is one of the reasons she is not yet employed. Being clear is just one step in the bold-move process, and not the only step. In my experience, spending time clarifying my idea increases my chances of getting it.

Let's explore this idea further. For instance, if you are single and you want a relationship, you know there are lots of other single people out there for you to date—potential boyfriends and girlfriends just waiting to be found, just like you. You can go on many dates, and good ones too, but which person is THE ONE you are searching for? The one meant just for you and with whom you could spend your future, maybe even choose to marry?

This same concept applies to anything we care about and want, and our next bold move toward attaining it. We can care about and want many things, and may potentially consider many of them as candidates for our next bold move. In fact, most of us have a gazillion things that interest us—I know I do, and my list, like yours, is long—so how do we narrow our list down to what we really, really want? How do we know what will juice and jazz us the most? Which is THE ONE idea that is the right bold move to put into play now? THE ONE worth pouring our time and energy into to create our future?

Many women have ways of thinking and acting that prevent them from moving forward with ease. Taking care of others before taking care of themselves, caring about what others think about their actions, and pleasing others around them are all obstacles women need to learn how to work through in order to act *and* feel good about getting what they want. Becoming clear about what you want requires a sense of personal power, as it requires women to consider their own needs as important, and not submerge them for the sake of pleasing others.

Masculine and Feminine Approaches to Getting Clear About What You Want

The masculine approach to getting clear about what you want is ready, aim, fire. Masculine energy is primarily interested in executing and being in action, and the masculine can find it challenging to first take the time to check in with feelings and intuition about the situation, or to reflect on what matters most. The masculine so wants to make a move, any move, just to be moving forward, that sometimes the right move can remain elusive. It takes time to get crystal clear before you can execute with precision. The masculine mind knows it is on the right track. The masculine values logical analysis and action over connecting the action to deeply held values or listening to the sounds of our inner feelings.

The feminine approach is just the opposite. Its method is ready, aim, listen to our internal signals, check our value system, then fire, maybe, if it feels right. The feminine can fall in love with an idea to the extent that the good feeling the idea brings becomes the all-consuming focus versus the execution. Feminine energy believes, *"If I love the idea enough, the execution will take care of itself."* The feminine values the good feeling that the connection to values creates. The feminine's heart knows it is on the right track. As wonderful as this quality is, without the active execution-and-fire principle the developed masculine side brings, execution suffers.

The masculine without the feminine executes quickly—often too quickly—creating a lot of activity, but personal satisfaction, reward, and long-term results suffer. The feminine without the masculine connects desire with values, but has trouble with razor-sharp clarity, and often execution suffers. The feminine heart clarifies loosely with an infinite time line, while the masculine mind clarifies sharply to get into action quickly.

As you can see, it's helpful to integrate both the masculine proclivity toward action and the feminine appetite for connectedness to what matters. If you are more oriented toward the masculine, it is critical to develop your feminine capacities and style, and vice versa. Make your next bold move with clarity and action, *and* connect it to what matters most to your heart and soul to give yourself a shot at getting it. Consider what masculine and feminine skills and capacities you need to develop, and then act accordingly!

Personally, I have had the most difficult time learning how to get clear about what I want, and I'm not really a wishy-washy type of person. When I get stuck and challenged, I resort to using my masculine side to figure it out first. The masculine side of me often sounds like I'm clear about what I want, especially when others hear me speak it out loud. But inside there are so many important pieces I haven't quite sorted through yet; I just sound like I know what I'm talking about. Getting clear about what you want seems easy, but like I said, it ain't necessarily so.

My husband says it's a lot like playing baseball and catching high flies in the outfield. When a ball comes your way, either you put up your baseball mitt and go all out to catch it, or you decide the ball is coming too fast or too hard and fear takes over. You think, "There is no way I can catch this ball." And guess what happens? You miss it, or you make a half-hearted effort to catch it. We all know the disappointment of watching someone miss a ball they really could have caught, and the sympathetic "Ohhh!" from the crowd. We all know on some level that that player is us, and we want them to give it their all—even if they end up missing it— just like our fans (our friends and family) want us to give it *our* all.

I think part of the reason I have trouble getting clear, and many of us have trouble, is that we use our primary approach (masculine or feminine) and don't incorporate the other less-developed approach into our thought process. We become afraid. What are we afraid of? We're afraid that it might be too hard, that we're not smart enough, that we don't have enough money, that we're too thin, too fat, too out of shape, too old, too young—you name it. We conclude that it is simply overwhelming and impossible to figure out how to do whatever it is before we even know *what* it is. In the face of our fear, everything seems big and unattainable.

Yes, we're afraid the ball will be too high, too fast, and too hard to catch. Writing this book was like that for me. I wanted to write, but the task of writing a book was too daunting to even consider that it could be possible at first. Here are some of the conversations I had with myself:

> *You're not an author. You don't know anything about writing a book. You don't have any connections or support in that arena. You're not even that good a writer! Remember that time when you were 26, and your boss told you that your business writing skills needed improving, and she marked up that memo with red pen corrections all over it? What if you tell people you're going to write a book and they laugh at you? Who would even want to read about what you have to say anyway? When do you think you are going to find the time to write?*

And so on. But then something happened—my feminine side felt a pull toward writing that I could not ignore. No matter how many times I tried to talk myself out of it and rationalize myself out of it, the idea kept showing up in different ways in my life. During my time-outs, my intuition kept circling back to the idea of writing a book, in spite of my strong reluctance. I even got an out-of-the-blue email from a publisher who said that a mutual friend of ours (whom I must have told I was thinking about writing) told him about the book. I couldn't believe that he was interested in my sending him the first three chapters as soon as they were done!

It's okay to be afraid. It's okay to not know how you will pull off this big or little idea of yours. It's okay to not even believe it is possible. If you want it, if you are clear about it, if your heart calls you forward, then eventually you have no choice but to say yes. And really, what do you have to lose? You didn't have it to begin with, and maybe the path to getting there will bring you wonderful things you never imagined. And maybe, just maybe, you'll be an author. Or living overseas. Or engaged to the person of your dreams. Or in a new job that makes your heart *and* your wallet sing. Or you'll start the business you've been dreaming about. Just put up your mitt. Don't think your way out of it. Know that you want to catch the ball that's coming your way. You don't even have to believe in yourself yet. Just put up your mitt.

Getting Started

To help you get started in identifying and getting even clearer about your next bold move, ask yourself the following questions. Ask your analytical mind if it likes the idea (masculine approach), and then ask your heart if it feels right (feminine approach).

Questions:
1. What do I really want?
2. What do I really care about?
3. What am I good at?
4. What's important to me?
5. Why am I here?
6. What is my passion? My life purpose? My spirit song?

While taking a class for entrepreneurs at Babson College a few years ago, I heard a great story that illustrated the importance of learning how to focus on what's most important.
Here goes: Two groups of ten students each participated in an experiment. Group 1 was told to walk down the street to a sporting goods store and look in the window for ten minutes. Group 2 was told to do the same thing, but to look for items related to water sports. Group 1, when asked to report on how many things they saw in the window, reported remembering an average of 15 items. Group 2, when asked the same question,

remembered an average of 25 items, and then remembered additional non–sporting goods equipment that was also in the window. Wow! Think about the implications of this study! The more we can focus on what we want, the better our chances of success in getting it. It's all about the clear focus.

Exercises and Activities

Write your answers in the spaces provided below.

- Make a list of things you really care about. What's most important to you?

- Now pick one thing from your list that you think and feel in this moment is THE ONE, and write it below in a clear next-bold-move statement. Write it as if it has already happened and is already true about you.

  Example:
  What I really care about is helping other people discover their gifts and talents to make their unique footprint in the world. My next-bold-move statement: I am the author of a best-selling book called **Your Next Bold Move**.*

- When someone listens, we can hear ourselves and our wants more clearly. Tell three people who are your biggest supporters your next bold move and notice if it sounds right to you, feels right, gives you joy, and maybe even gives you goose bumps. What was it like to share what you want?

* By the time you read this next-bold-move statement I will be an author, but in this moment I am still just a girl writing at my desk. When I declared that I was an author for the first time, I did not really believe it and thought it was a crazy thing to say. So don't worry if you feel dubious and wonder if it will ever really come true. My rule of thumb here is "fake it 'til you make it." Try not to make a face when you say it. Try not to discount or take back what you say. Try not to make any kind of disclaimer at all. Just be courageous and speak boldly. The Universe will hear your voice and your commitment and will start to conspire on your behalf.

Brainstormers to Get Clear About What You Want

1. Bold moves need to be connected to what we care about.
2. What do *you* really want? Care about? What matters most?
3. Which desire should you act upon?
4. The world is full of potential boyfriends and girlfriends—which is the one for you?
5. Just because you love something doesn't mean you can make a living doing it, or that you should—possibly, but not necessarily. You can turn your love into your living or your hobby.
6. Ask someone to listen with a quiet mind to what you really want and to give you feedback.
7. When we are listened to, we can hear our own needs and wants more clearly.
8. Does your next bold move jazz you and make your heart sing?
9. What do you love?
10. How do you know what you want?

Summary

Rumi, one of the most influential Persian poets of the 13th century, said, "Let yourself be silently drawn by the stronger pull of what you really love." And seven hundred years or so later, I have to say I agree with him.

Some examples of clear next-bold-move statements, made by participants in a recent *"Next Bold Move"* workshop who got clear about what they cared about:

- I want to live and work overseas next year.
- I want to leave my job and get a job in the fine wine industry selling fine wines to restaurants.
- I want to write my memoir.
- I want to go to Paris and live for a month.
- I want to fall in love and get engaged in the next two years.

- I want to write a children's book.
- I want to get myself physically healthy in the next 12 months.
- I want to increase my business so much that I have to hire two employees to handle all the new clients.

The sixth step in creating your next bold move is to *Surround Yourself with Extreme Support.* Those who support us buoy us, and those who do not drag us down and make us doubt ourselves. To *Surround Yourself with Extreme Support* is not an option—it's a requirement.

Stay tuned for Chapter 6, *Surround Yourself with Extreme Support.*

Additional Resources

Here is a list of things you can read, listen to, or watch to inspire you to *Get Clear About What You Want.*

Books:

Wishcraft by Barbara Sher

The Heart Aroused: Poetry and the Preservation of Soul in Corporate America by David Whyte

Videos:

How I Harnessed the Wind: William Kamkwamba
http://blog.ted.com/2009/09/23/how_i_harnessed/

Britain's Got Talent: **Janey Cutler**
http://www.youtube.com/watch?v=JAwOZvvGsRs

Music:

"Over the Rainbow" by Eva Cassidy

"Strength, Courage & Wisdom" by India Arie

Chapter 6

Surround Yourself with Extreme Support

The dictionary says the word *extreme* is an adjective that means
"reaching a high or the highest degree; very great." To *Surround
Yourself with Extreme Support*, the focus is the adjective itself:
Extreme. Great. Tremendous. Intense. Maximum. Ultimate. You
get the idea, right? Here's the thing. We cannot achieve our goals
alone, and certainly not the really big goals like making a bold
move. We need support, and a lot of it. More than you *think* you
need. More than you are comfortable with. A *lot* more. Extreme.

Women don't typically have enough support in their lives. They
don't want to bother others or impose on them, and as a result,
women often don't ask for help. Men typically think they can do
it all by themselves, and frequently feel it is expected of them to
do so. Therefore, asking for help might make them appear weak
or incompetent. As a result, many of us wait until we are in crisis
before we cry out for help. Unfortunately, by that time we are
either truly desperate or at least feeling like a train wreck.

In my work as an executive coach and advisor, I have had the
opportunity to work with many corporate executives and senior
managers. The best leaders I have had the privilege to work with
know that in order to run their organizations most effectively,
they need the help of many sounding boards. They receive
invaluable support from individuals inside the organization who
can provide insider intelligence about what's going on. They also
find it beneficial to obtain external support from people like me
who will give them a perspective they cannot get from the
people inside their organizations. The internal people, because
they are impacted by every decision made and are often too
close to the issues, are not able to be objective enough to give
totally honest feedback. Whether or not you are an executive
who works in a corporation, the message is the same: surround
yourself with extreme support. Bring an outsider's objectivity to

your situation, while you surround yourself with those who you know have your best interest at heart and can help you work through your toughest challenges.

There is nothing effective about going it alone, and there is clearly little value to be gained by waiting until we are in crisis to ask for help. Going it alone usually takes longer, for starters. You can only look at a given situation through your own eyes. Being limited to our own perspective means we miss out on the opportunity to have our thinking challenged or to be inspired by someone other than ourselves. Having this input on a consistent basis can help us reach beyond what we think is possible for ourselves, catapulting us to new heights.

The masculine way to move through the world is to go it alone. This path is often referred to as the hero's journey. Solo. The feminine way to move through the world is through connection, relationship, and community. Whether we are oriented more toward the masculine or the feminine, for some reason we seem to think we can do or should do it alone. This belief does not really work or serve our needs in the long run. When we ask for and receive support from others, we are inspired and juiced by each other. We are able to find our own courage as we are buoyed up by each other. In addition, the new ideas we get from others can often be invaluable.

I would not have started this book as soon as I did without a number of people telling me to go for it, and a friend offering to barter with me and edit my writing. The support of my husband was also critical. When I asked him, in a moment of incredible bravery (okay, so maybe I held my breath because I was so scared to ask), he agreed to leave our vacation house for two hours in the morning every day to give me the space I needed when I was first starting to write.

You might be wondering what extreme support might look like for you. It's sometimes hard to know, especially when everything seems just fine at the moment or you are used to going it alone.

At different stages of our projects, businesses, or bold moves, we might need different kinds of support. Ask yourself, *What do I need now that I don't currently have, and what do I predict I might need down the road?*

There are two kinds of support: personal and professional. Professional support includes a good network, coaching, mentoring, and products or services that support where you are and where you are headed. I have two coaches who provide me with extreme professional support for my business ventures; one supports my business development and one coaches me to enhance myself as a leader in my field. In addition to my coaches, I have a graphic designer; a webmaster; an instructional designer for my leadership training programs; trainers, coaches, and consultants who work with me; a friend in the TV business who helps me develop and create new ideas for my TV show, *Your Next Bold Move*; a mastermind group to keep me on track professionally; an advisory board; and a board of directors. As you can see, my list is long! Well, it's *extreme*! I cannot imagine functioning at my desired level in my business (or in my life, for that matter) without this high level of expertise and such a wonderful support structure.

Personal support includes the personal relationships in your life: family, friends, acquaintances, neighbors, and members of various communities. Out of all these relationships, you have to determine who you want on your A team—the people who support you and help you soar, and not those who make you doubt yourself or feel smaller or less competent. Who would *you* rather be with? People who support you or those that don't? The health, fitness, and wellness industry is built on this concept of extreme support. Personal fitness training, diet and nutrition programs, and career counseling are examples of entire industries built around the concept of extreme support to help those who want to obtain their goals.

Getting Started

The first step, although not always the easiest, is to clean up your personal relationships and surround yourself with those people you want close to you during this time of making your next bold move. This means you will need to dissolve or minimize relationships that no longer support you. This can be a very difficult, but nonetheless important, process. When I started my women's organization, I announced my idea at a family dinner party. My siblings laughed their heads off and my husband made a snide remark. I felt deflated because I thought my idea was so wonderful, but they thought I was crazy and told me so. Of course I did not divorce my family, but I was pretty certain at the time that they were in the non-supporter camp. So, for quite some time, I dramatically reduced how much I talked to them about my plans and how I was progressing. (P.S. My family isn't laughing anymore, since our women's organization has grown to include over 500 women after many years of running personal leadership retreats.)

A few years ago, my coach asked me to clean house of the relationships that no longer supported me. To be honest, I had a difficult time looking at my personal friendships and deciding which ones were not really working for me anymore. For instance, I had some friendships I developed with other parents when my kids were young. Those friendships served me then, but seemed less vibrant now. They were great friends to hang with when I sat at the soccer field for hours or waited at the dance studio for class to end, but now it seemed like I was the only one expending the effort to stay in touch. I also had some friends to whom I felt I was giving more and more without getting much in return. One friend in particular was always in crisis. I felt like I was her therapist, listening to story after story about her complaints. I realized I was spending a lot of time taking care of her needs and wants without the reciprocity I needed. Out of habit and comfort of some kind, we had remained friends even though our relationship felt uncomfortably one-sided to me. I decided, if I told myself the truth, that relationships like this one were no longer supporting me. In a gentle and gradual way, I began to spend less and less time with these friends, and this choice gave me the emotional space I needed to develop new relationships that were more balanced, where I felt equally supported.

I really do feel like I am married to the man of my dreams. So, when my husband didn't like the idea of my spending more time working and developing my women's organization, I was pretty upset. Even though I knew he loved me, I did not feel supported, and I was upset by his consistent remarks that he thought I was wasting my time on something that did not have any redeeming value—to him it was just a bunch of women getting together to talk. My friend Elaine put it all in perspective for me one day when she said, "I don't do all my grocery shopping at one store. I go to Trader Joe's for some things and Whole Foods and Stop and Shop for other things. I don't expect I will get everything I need at one store." I realized that although I wished I had my husband's support for this project, I didn't really need it. I could go "shopping" for support for this endeavor from other sources and minimize the amount I talked with him about what I was doing, for now. The strategy I adopted from Elaine helped me gain perspective on the stress I was putting on my marriage and on myself.

So, my pearl of wisdom: *Don't make yourself crazy looking for support or demanding it from those in your life who aren't really able or willing to provide it.* Don't expect one person, no matter who they are, to provide the exact and perfect kind of support in every area where you have needs. Support cannot come in the form of one person, even if they are the love of your life. That's just not the way it works. If someone is not your biggest supporter, face reality and accept what you can from them based on what they are capable of offering, and go elsewhere for the rest. A key to getting what you need is being able to appropriately shift your expectations. Thank goodness, it all worked out fine in the end with my husband. He got used to me doing women's organization work, and over time we both saw that there was room for my love and passion for my work with women and with my consulting practice without jeopardizing my financial contribution to the family.

So here is my advice: *Surround yourself with relationships that support you to the nth degree.* People who think you rock. Friends who think you are special and love you for who you are. A partner, spouse, or loved one who loves you and is doing their best to support you. When my husband and extended family laughed at the idea of my starting a women's organization, I knew I needed to go and find my support for this endeavor elsewhere. So I asked a few friends and colleagues if they would be willing to act as an advisory group to help me brainstorm, to help grow and develop the idea. This was extreme support since there were seven of them! The Magic Council, as we call ourselves, has been a tremendous resource and an *extreme*-ly supportive board of advisors for the past four years. When my family laughed, I cried inside. But my board gave me the "atta-girl" courage and support to plan and develop what was, at the time, my next bold move. Today, it is a very successful organization dedicated to birthing women's dreams and to supporting women as they make their next bold move.

Here are some ideas for developing extreme support:
1. Network until you find the people who feel right to support your next step.
2. Hire a coach.
3. Get a mentor.
4. Clean house in your personal relationships.

Exercises and Activities

Write your answers in the spaces provided on the next couple of pages.

- What kind of personal and/or professional support do you think you need in order to make your next bold move? Think about different levels of support, including networking, coaching, mentoring, products, or services.

- Make a list of your biggest personal and professional supporters.

- Whom do you know who might be a good coach to move you toward your next bold move?

- Is there someone who might be a good mentor for you at this time? Someone who has already walked the road you are embarking on and can help guide you?

- In what relationships do you need to shift the balance (more or less) to get more support? What specifically needs to shift?

- If you were going to do *one thing* that would make the greatest positive impact on your being supported, what do you think it would be?

Brainstormers to Surround Yourself with Extreme Support

1. Believing we can or should do it by ourselves is not useful.
2. Working within a community serves us and buoys us up.
3. Extreme support means people who see us as great.
4. Extreme support includes products and services.
5. Examine whom you want to support you in the future you are building.
6. Choose supporters who will NOT give up on you.
7. Coaches and mentors will ask you hard questions that you cannot ask yourself.
8. Coaches and mentors will help you dream bigger and imagine beyond what you think is possible.
9. Offer support to others; learn to become a two-way support street.

Summary

It is essential for all of us to proactively put a support structure in place. The support we ask for and receive will help us gain confidence in ourselves, develop our capacities, and enhance our skill sets. We all need personal sounding boards with whom to try out new ideas and evaluate our results. Support can help us gain traction on our ideas, keeping us engaged when we get tired, on track when we get distracted, and accountable to the relentless pursuit of our ideas, giving them roots and strengthening our creativity, commitment, and energy.

All good ideas come from an ongoing sequence of small sparks—and the first one is usually not all that good. Thanks to the support we surround ourselves with, we get sparked with more ideas to help us create projects and ultimately turn our dreams into reality. In his book *Making Ideas Happen*, Scott Belsky says, "...sharing ideas significantly increases the odds of ideas gaining momentum and ultimately happening. Creative professionals and entrepreneurs alike claim that they become more committed to their ideas after telling people about them. When your ideas are known by many, they are more likely to be refined, and you are more likely to stay focused on them."

Extreme support is a requirement in making your next bold move, so start creating new ways to be *extreme*-ly supported.

The seventh step in creating your next bold move is to *Gather in Purposeful Community*. Purposeful community is the community of like-minded people that you select who are related to your next bold move, who help you generate fresh ideas and move forward.

Stay tuned for Chapter 7, *Gather in Purposeful Community*.

Additional Resources

Here is a list of things that I read, listen to, or watch to inspire me to surround myself with extreme support.

Books:

The Best Year of Your Life: Dream It, Plan It, Live It by Debbie Ford

Making Ideas Happen by Scott Belsky

Transitions: Making Sense of Life's Changes by William Bridges

The Art of Possibility: Transforming Professional and Personal Life
by Rosamund Stone Zander and Ben Zander

Websites:

Meetup: http://www.meetup.com/

Women's Retreats
http://visionquestconsulting.com/events/

Corporate Women's Leadership Programs and Workshops
http://visionquestconsulting.com/womens-leadership/

Videos:

Validation
http://www.youtube.com/watch?v=Cbk980jV7Ao

Music:

"Just the Way You Are" by Bruno Mars

"This is My Now" by Jordin Sparks

Chapter 7

Gather in Purposeful Community

The feminine side of me loves connection and community. I
heard somewhere that "community is a place where your gifts
are received." I love the idea that the right community is a place
where we can be our true selves, because it supports us with all
of our strengths, gifts, and talents. I want to distinguish this step
from the previous chapter, *Surround Yourself with Extreme
Support*, which refers to surrounding yourself with the right
people, products, and services that support your next bold move.
Gather in Purposeful Community is specifically related to
gathering a community of like-minded people around you who
are connected through sharing a common focus, identity, or
vision.

Miriam-Webster's Collegiate Dictionary refers to community as "a
gathering of people with common interests." In order to make
your next bold move, I believe it makes a huge difference in your
capacity to move forward if you have the support and guidance
of the right targeted community, where you feel comfortable and
challenged in a way that supports you. This powerful resource
will provide you with an infusion of fresh ideas, feedback, and a
new perspective for yourself, as well as:

- Mentoring
- Cheering you onward and upward
- Picking you up when you falter
- Providing you with a reality check
- Witnessing your successes and challenges
- Providing advice, resources, and a network as you
  need help

In my professional life, I belong to a mastermind group of
entrepreneurs who are building consulting practices similar to
mine. We meet every other month to share best practices and

ideas around how to continue to grow and expand, while providing the level of service and excellence we deem critical to our success. Once a year I gather with other seasoned and master-level executive coaches, also to share best practices and new ideas. These two communities of practice give me a sense of reassurance that I have a place to go to get help, support, *and* a wonderful infusion of fresh ideas to incorporate into my work.

When I was first getting into the coaching profession, I gathered with other individuals who had the same coaching interest that I did. We were a great comfort to and resource for each other, as well as to help each other in the growth of our coaching businesses.

Being in purposeful community gives us the actual experience of support and relieves some of the pressure of having to go it alone. My women's organization is just that kind of community. It's a place where women can be supported, inspired, celebrated, and provided with resources and information to keep them on track toward what's next in their lives.

Getting Started

The first step is to find people who are committed to the same values or interests that you have. This type of community is for the sole purpose of moving forward with your next bold move. It could form around your own personal Next bold move theme; for example, if you were thinking of going into business for yourself, the group might be a group of small business entrepreneurs. It could be related to a specific profession; if you were thinking of going into the wine distribution business, it might be a wine-tasting class. Or, if your next bold move is related to money, you might consider joining an investment group. You might join a group whose focus is on career paths, if your bold move involves changing careers. Your primary goal should be targeting the idea that you are trying to bring into being. This is not about just gathering friends together, although your community could have friends in it. Focus on creating or joining the community that has both what you want and what you need.

A few years ago, I became interested in developing my feminine style, and in developing women's leadership programs as a new product for my company to offer to organizations wanting to enhance women's leadership. To learn more about women and their leadership styles, even though I'm not a regular temple going kind of girl, I joined my temple's sisterhood community, and I started meeting with groups of women in my home. I also sought out and met with corporations who were running women's leadership initiatives, and over the last four years I have concentrated on attending women's conferences. The idea was to immerse myself in women and to gain an understanding of women's leadership styles.

For the past year, my bold move has been writing this book. I'd been talking to many people about whether to go with a publishing house or go the self-published route when I realized that it might be useful to join a community of writers. This community gave me advice on which way to go and the pros and cons of each to help me make the best decision for myself. Similarly, my friend Susan wanted to change jobs after 25 years in the same field. I suggested she join a career group whose focus is helping its members figure out what their next career move might be. When my colleague Lynne wanted to get in shape physically, she joined a gym and a zumba class. Ten years ago, I wanted to find my voice and learn how to speak with more confidence and power, and I thought singing would help. I joined a community choir, and I've been singing with the Mystic Chorale ever since. My friend Beth is a runner, and she runs each morning with a group of neighbors who are all runners. You get the idea, right?

The Masculine and the Feminine

The masculine approach is to check in with your logical mind to assess whether this is the right group for you. Do they have members who already have accomplished what you want to accomplish, or are they striving toward similar goals to yours? Both can be useful.

Many women have a keen sense that doing it alone would not be as effective as having the support and collaboration that these types of communities offer. Often men think they can do pretty much anything themselves, which I call the "lone cowboy" or the "hero" archetype, and they don't typically reach out for support and collaboration even if they think these attributes are necessary for them to be successful. The relief one gets from being with others who are up to the same thing you are is well worth whatever it might take to crawl out of your comfort zone.

Personally, there are times I just want to be with others who have accomplished what I want to accomplish. Like the time when I was 20 and I attended a tennis clinic. I really didn't want to be with the beginners, even though I *was* a beginner, because I knew I wouldn't get better very fast by playing with someone as bad as or even worse than I was! On the other hand, I did wonder why someone better than I would want to play with a beginner—but if I could have found that person, I felt certain they would have raised my game quickly.

I once joined a small mastermind group because the members in it had a history of building businesses and then taking them public. At the time, I thought this was something I wanted to do. I stayed with the group for three years and learned through our work together that I did want to build a business, but that I did not want to perform the kind of requirements necessary to take it public. This was an important turning point in my business, and it informed me which way to move forward. An important assessment of the group you are exploring should be whether they can contribute to you and your next bold move. If you find yourself in a group that doesn't seem to fit who you are or where you are headed, cut your losses as quickly as possible. It's pretty easy to determine if you are obtaining value, although I recommend you try it out for a few sessions to make certain you are not jumping to a wrong conclusion too quickly.

Sometimes it is helpful to be with others who are in the same boat. An example might be a networking group. These groups often have members who are looking to change their careers or to get new jobs. They have workshops and speakers who help you write a powerful resume and give you techniques for job searches. It is often reassuring to be with others who are in the same situation, so you at least don't feel so alone, and you receive ideas you would not have thought of by yourself. I find that in these communities you can commiserate and share success strategies with others as you move forward in your work goals.

The feminine approach is to check in with your heart to see if a group feels like it is full of people you could enjoy spending time with. Do they speak the same language that you do, or a language that you want to speak? Do they invite you in and make you feel honored, respected, and a welcome addition to their group? Does your heart dance a little jig when you think about getting together with them, or when you are on your way to meet with them? Do you trust them? Do they come from a place of contribution and caring about you as a person versus being in competition with you? Do you feel connected to the community in a way that is joyful and easy for you? This is the intuitive feminine way of determining whether your heart *and* your gut feel at home in this community, for now.

In addition to using the feminine approach to select your group, you also need to use the masculine approach to analyze rationally whether you think this group can give you what you want. The masculine can tolerate a little discomfort if the group has what you really want, as you learn to settle into a new reality for yourself that will be beneficial and bring you many rewards.

Your wants, needs, and goals are an ever-changing landscape, and you will have many chances and choices to *Gather in Purposeful Community* as you move toward your next bold move.

Exercises and Activities

Write your answers in the spaces provided below.

- Make a list of any communities you are aware of that you might be interested in checking out or joining.

- Informally interview 3–5 people who already have accomplished what you have designated as your next bold move, and ask them what groups they belong to and would recommend for you.

- What does your intuition tell you about what kind of purposeful community you need at this time?

Brainstormers to Gather in Purposeful Community

1. Gather in intentional and purposeful community.
2. Believe in yourself enough to know what you want.
3. It's an opportunity to both get ideas around the things you don't know and share the things you do know.
4. Mentoring, cheering you on, a reality check.
5. Take the journey with others.
6. You can't overdo this type of support.
7. Create a next bold move brain team.
8. What kind of purposeful community would serve your next bold step?
9. Is there something missing that you could add?
10. Put yourself in a situation where you can be unconditionally supported.
11. Witness successes.
12. Not doing it alone is key.
13. Connection.
14. Support network with heart and head—the feminine and the masculine.
15. Look for talents that you need.
16. Know when it's over and time for you to resign.
17. Form a group focused on a particular task, to do the work itself.
18. Gathering together doesn't have to be local/physical, you can use the phone or Skype.

Summary

Here's what I discovered in my own quest for getting supported through various communities of practice over the years: immersion is the key. Immerse and surround yourself with your dream, with what's next, and with others who are on a similar path. Start with one community or group, and maybe more than one, that will help keep you on track to launch, execute, and sustain your efforts.

Don't do it alone. I believe in being in community, surrounded and supported by others. I believe that finding the right communities to support you where you are at this moment, and where you are headed, is crucial. It is so much easier when we have help and others inspire and encourage us to reach a bit further for ourselves. And in turn, sometimes without knowing it, we inspire and encourage others by simply being who we are, and by making the choices we make. When I jog with my husband and others, I go a bit further and a bit faster because they inspire me to reach beyond what I think is possible for me. And that's the point, isn't it—to find a community of practice that inspires you to reach a bit beyond what you might do by yourself?

As His Holiness the Dalai Lama noted, "Educating the intellect alone is a prescription for disaster. We must also be educating the heart." Using both your masculine *and* your feminine styles and approaches together to determine which purposeful community is right for you will bring you closer to finding the perfect community to support your next bold move.

Now that you have developed your purposeful community; it is time to move your bold move from the idea stage into reality. Chapter 8 will outline the most effective way for you to move into action and execute your idea.

Stay tuned for Chapter 8, *Generate Some STEAM.*

Additional Resources

Here is a list of things that I read, listen to, or watch to inspire me to *Gather in Purposeful Community.*

Books:

Finding Your Way in a Wild New World: Reclaim Your True Nature to Create the Life You Want by Martha Beck

Walk Out Walk On: A Learning Journey into Communities Daring to Live the Future Now by Margaret Wheatley and Deborah Frieze

The Abundant Community: Awakening the Power of Families and Neighborhoods by John McKnight and Peter Block

The Necessary Revolution: How Individuals and Organizations Are Working Together to Create a Sustainable World by Peter Senge, Bryan Smith, Nina Kruschwitz, Joe Laur, and Sara Schley

Videos:

"Banc Sabadelle"
http://www.youtube.com/watch_popup?v=GBaHPND2QJg

Perputuum Jazzile: "Africa"
http://www.youtube.com/watch?v=yjbpwlqp5Qw

Opera Company of Philadelphia's Random Act of Culture: "Hallelujah!"
http://www.youtube.com/watch?v=wp_RHnQ-jgU

Music:

"Good Life" by OneRepublic

"Respect" by Aretha Franklin

Chapter 8

Generate Some STEAM

Last night I got a message inside my fortune cookie that gave me a dose of inspiration about this chapter. It said, "Somewhere deep inside, we all can fly."

This chapter is about action. Taking your next bold move out for a test drive. Taking flight. The approach I recommend is to *Generate Some STEAM.*

> **S**tep into action.
> **T**weak—analyze what's working and adjust what isn't.
> **E**xecute and experiment.
> **A**ct again.
> **M**easure your results each step along the way.

STEAM is the process of action and execution in which you can effectively move yourself forward one step at a time toward your next bold move. It's the deliberate action and forward movement that makes this step different from the others. Now you are putting into action what you have been preparing for throughout all the other steps. The size of the step is less important than the fact that you take a step in the first place, and then continue to take another step and then another, keeping yourself in constant forward motion. This chapter is about *being* in action—not just thinking about it or planning it, but actually stepping out and seeing how it goes.

To turn your idea into reality, you must eventually stop thinking and, with a plan in mind, act. Your plan can be as simple as knowing what you want, which we clarified in Chapter 5. Now you are ready to execute the details to move toward getting it. Moving into action also requires outlining the specific steps that are required to successfully implement your plan. You don't have to take big, GIGANTIC, awe-inspiring steps; just take one step at a time—even a baby step— and that can be just perfect.

I sometimes imagine that the Universe somehow feels our steps and creates momentum under our feet to inspire us to take another step the next day. Mike Dooley is CEO of www.tut.com (Totally Unique Thoughts), an online resource that sends daily inspirational email messages called "Notes from the Universe" to help members make their dreams come true. According to TUT, the Universe says, "Never stop asking for help, trying new directions, responding to conditions, innovating and evolving. For every step you take, The Universe takes 10,000 on your behalf." And, "The secret behind miracles is that the one performing them begins without any knowledge whatsoever of exactly how they will succeed, yet still they begin. When you move, I move. Once again, action wins the day." If what Mike Dooley says is true, taking just one step at a time has the Universe very busy on our behalf. Maybe we have to do less than we think to get a big result.

A few years ago I went to an Entrepreneurial Thought and Action course taught by Len Schlesinger, president of Babson College, and Charlie Kiefer, president of Innovation Associates. They propose that the most successful entrepreneurs figure out what they want and then take small steps with what they currently know and have at their disposal. They've also co-authored a book on the same subject, *Just Start: Take Action, Embrace Uncertainty, Create the Future*, in which Schlesinger and Kiefer recommend small steps in favor of big leaps to minimize risk and build from there based on what you discover. Len says, "It's a matter of acting your way through versus thinking your way through. You can only generate evidence by acting, so take action to create the evidence. Step and learn, then step and learn some more." I really love their approach; it seems less daunting to me. We can all take a step and learn from it, like an experiment, then make another action. Step. Learn. Step. Learn. Little by little, you continue to move forward, one step and one discovery at a time.

Identifying your first step seems like a reasonable and potentially easy place to start, don't you think? After trying out this first step, analyze how it worked and make some tweaks if needed before you take your next reasonable and potentially easy step forward. Execute first one step, and then another. If it works, keep going. If it doesn't, learn from the process and try something else. If you treat it like an experiment, you may find yourself turning your next bold move from an idea into a reality. And that's called an adventure.

Here's an example of my own step-and-learn process. Many years ago, my bold move was switching careers without any relevant background or much work experience. I was 26 years old, and I wanted to leave my elementary school teaching job and move into a new career. The hard part was I didn't really know what I wanted to do next. The only thing I was certain of was that I did not want to teach fifth grade for the rest of my life, even though I really loved kids and loved teaching. So, I decided to take action.

Step 1. My first step, after realizing I wanted to work in a people-centric job in some capacity, was to sign up for a master's degree in counseling psychology at a local college part time, while working full-time as a teacher. So far, so good.

Learn from Step 1. One day I realized that everyone in my psych class was headed for social work or mental health jobs, and I was expected to do the same. These professions did not interest me all that much, so much to my advisor's dismay and discouragement, I started to explore what else I could do with my degree.

Step 2. I explored career options for counseling psychology majors by talking to my teachers. I talked to people in the field of human resources, conducting informational interviews with them about the field so I could learn more about their specific jobs.

Learn from Step 2. From my interviews, I realized I wanted to move into human resources. Eventually, I ended up as a management trainee working in a big Boston bank in their human resources department. It was an excellent career move and I was a happy girl. And it all started with Step 1, deciding to go to graduate school.

Sometimes imagining our next bold move is so daunting that we get scared, think we cannot do it, and ultimately believe it is not possible—no way. But by shifting our focus to knowing what we want (even though we are uncertain how we will get there or if we will ever arrive at all) and just focusing on one step at a time, we realize it can be done. We can succeed. We can take a step. And then, just one more step. Just like in *The Wizard of Oz*: follow, follow, follow, follow, follow the yellow brick road...

My husband, who was a runner when we met, taught me how to jog. I remember the brilliant running technique he taught me, so that I wouldn't be overwhelmed trying to jog distances that seemed impossible to me as a beginner: *Don't look for the finish line, just keep your eyes on the road and just jog to the first telephone pole. Focus on reaching the telephone pole. Once you reach it, just jog to the next telephone pole. Don't overwhelm yourself by thinking you have to jog two miles. Just go to one pole and then to the next.* That mental game has served me well with running and also with making my next bold move. When I look at the things I want, they can appear impossible and overwhelming, but if I just look to make the next step to the next telephone pole, they don't seem as daunting. On a good day, they even seem doable. And so they are.

The Masculine and the Feminine

The masculine way to *Generate Some STEAM* is by being in action and staying in action through the use of personal drive and power with an orientation toward results. Making things happen, being productive, and executing is the focus for the masculine. My fitness trainer says, "Let's kick butt!" She employs the masculine approach where the focus is, "Let's get it done in a powerful way." It's a great style to have in your execution toolbox when the situation requires a *go for it* attitude. The masculine creates a strategy and moves toward the designated goal with drive and determination to get the job done. It's an action-oriented and very effective approach.

The feminine style uses intuition, empathy, nourishment, and play to move forward. The focus is on connection. The feminine approach also wants results, but not at the expense of what matters most—creativity, vitality, relationships, and caring. The feminine approach uses *power with* versus the masculine approach of *power over.* The feminine way is values driven and includes relatedness, collaboration, and purpose-centered actions.

Combining the action orientation of the masculine and the values-first focus of the feminine is a win-win formula for executing anything and everything. Learn to weave both the masculine and feminine together as you use your intuition and your mind first to create, then to execute. To that end, don't plug in so fast in the morning when you wake up. Go exercise. Go meditate. Journal. Write. Give your mind a vacation first, then work.

> Don't open the door to the study
> and begin reading.
> Take down a musical instrument.
> Let the beauty we love be what we do.
> There are hundreds of ways to kneel and
> kiss the ground.
>
> —Mevlana Jelaluddin
> Rumi (1207–73)

Interrupting the pattern of leading with drive and mind if you are more masculine-oriented will help you connect to what matters most and, as a result, will make you happier. If your style is more feminine, laid back, and creative, you probably need help putting your goals into an action plan, and actually moving forward with them versus *thinking* about them and creating new ideas instead of implementing. Step, baby step. One step at a time, but get started.

Getting Started

State your next bold move and answer the questions below to determine if you should go forward with it or not. You must answer *yes* to each question below, or the chances of your being successful are not all that likely.

1. Is your bold move doable?
   In other words, can it be done? Is it market feasible? Is it technically possible? Is it an idea that can be done? Or, is it just a cool, interesting idea?
2. Can you do it?
   Is this something you can actually do? Or, is someone else with a certain skill set actually the better match to do this?
3. Will your next bold move be meaningful to you?
   Is this idea something that aligns with your values, with your life purpose, with who you are and the contribution you want to make in the world?
4. Is your next bold move worth doing?
   Will it give you financial, emotional, or personal rewards or benefits?
5. Do you really, unequivocally want to do it?
   Do you love the idea of doing this or does it seem like a pain in the neck, too troublesome, and maybe not really worth your time in the long run? Does it seem like it will be incredibly fun?

Assuming you answered *yes* to all of these questions, it's time to get started and execute your first step. Before we move on, let's walk through these questions with an entrepreneurial idea my husband and I had the other night so you can see how it works with a real-life situation.

Chris and I were imagining a potential new business idea where we would provide carpentry, electrical, and home maintenance services to elderly people who needed help maintaining their homes, or else they would have to move to a nursing or assisted-living facility. Here is how we walked through the questions above.

1. Is it doable?
   Yes, this is an idea that we believe can easily be done, and there is a great market need for this service as the population continues to age and people increasingly want to stay in their own homes.
2. Can you do it?
   Yes, Chris could manage the business, get the clients, market the idea, and recruit people to do the work. We already know three guys who would love this idea and who are available to do the work as a starting point.
3. Will it be meaningful?
   Yes, it is meaningful to us as we would be helping people and making their dream of staying in their homes possible. It's a wonderful service to provide and aligns well with our idea of giving back to the world by helping others and helping to make their lives more comfortable.
4. Is it worth doing?
   It would give us a great deal of emotional and personal satisfaction; however, we got stuck when we got to the question, "Will it give you financial rewards or benefits?" Try as we might, we could not figure out how to make enough money to make a living—even a modest one—with this idea. We realized that there is a market rate for this kind of work, and if we wanted to get paid for our time working on the development, marketing, and management of the business, it would be too cost prohibitive for people to hire us, or we would have to pay our contractors well below market rate. We didn't think

we could easily attract quality contractors at such a low pay rate. We also wondered about the feasibility of managing so many contractors. We estimated that in order to make a decent living with the margins we would need, we would need 120 contractors all working full time, consistently. This seemed unrealistic. Suddenly, this great idea we started with really did not seem all that possible for the level of success we would want.

We tried crafting a few different business models before giving up on the idea, but continued to circle back to the same conclusion. "Ah well," we thought, and aborted our idea. Not all good ideas are good business ideas, as you can see by our example, so use these questions to help you determine the right ones for you to move forward and act on.

For those of you with a business background, you might be wondering, "Where does the strategic business plan come into the picture?" When you are further along in the process, you will need a business plan, a financial plan, business goals and objectives, and a structure and process to make your plan succeed. But not yet. This step, *Generate Some STEAM*, is the prerequisite and introduction to the action phase of your next bold move. Creating a business outline for your next bold move is important, as you will need to specify how your business will operate and create and deliver value—but only when you have some success under your belt and have determined you want to continue moving forward.

As step and learn, we must measure our results. Why? A less intimidating way of saying this is, *Are you getting what you want?* Some questions you can ask yourself are:

- What results did you get that were linked to your goals?
- If you were not exactly on track, what and where was the gap?
- What ideas do you have to close the gap and get yourself back on track?

The inspiration to generate ideas comes easily to most of us, but the inspiration to take action is more rare. I know I sometimes keep going with something because I fall in love with the idea. When that happens I don't *want* a reality check. However, I know that it's great to have fun and even better to have fun while reaching my goals.

Here's an example. This recently happened to me when I was producing my TV show, *Your Next Bold Move*. While interviewing a potential guest for the show, she asked me how much the show was costing me to produce. Her inquiry was part of a "measuring success" question. I knew I was spending money each month, but I had never added it up, and I was shocked to discover the answer was $500 per month. I decided right then that from now on I would need sponsorships to help me cover the show costs. After two years of producing shows, the out-of-pocket expenses were really adding up. I had been so focused on how to make the show better and more impactful that I had neglected to measure the financial aspect, basing all my satisfaction on how the show was expanding and growing and how much fun I was having. I recognize the importance of these other success factors, but neglecting the financial aspect was an oversight that needed due consideration in order for the show to sustain itself over the long term.

Exercises and Activities

Answer the questions below to help you *Generate Some STEAM* more successfully.

- For every idea you want to realize, you must capture and highlight your action steps. Write down three things you want to have happen in the next 12–18 months.

- Make a list of the number of steps that are required in the next 30–60 days to move forward with each idea.

- List five or six obstacles or problems you currently face or imagine you will encounter in the process of getting what you want. In other words, what might stop you from getting what you want?

- Ask 3–5 people to listen to your ideas, the steps you think you might like to take, and the obstacles you may encounter, and to give you potential solutions to the obstacles. Write down every idea and suggestion they give you, and then sift through which ones make the most sense to you.

Brainstormers to Generate Some STEAM

1. If this project, idea, business, or service met my dreams, what would be accomplished?
2. What do I need to do to get out of my own way?
3. What support do I need and in what form in the next 30–60 days?
4. You must have a plan, even if only a next step.
5. One step at a time is perfect.
6. The Universe feels you step and transforms your inertia into momentum.
7. 5 Questions—you have to answer all five with yes's or make a change somewhere:
    a. Is it doable?
    b. Can you do it?
    c. Do you really want to do it? (Will it be meaningful to me?)
    d. Is it worth doing?
    e. Is it fun? (Will it bring me joy?)
8. Take a step and see how it feels—keep or tweak?
9. Timetable: If I don't have results by _____, I won't keep doing it the same way.
10. List three things you want in the next 12 months.
11. What steps will you need to take in the next 30 days?
12. What obstacles get in the way of your getting what you want?
13. What are some possible solutions?

Summary

Transforming your ideas into your next bold move can be messy. In the process of transforming from a caterpillar into a butterfly, the caterpillar becomes a mess of decay. Deepak Chopra calls this decay a "nutritive soup" because of the opportunity and possibility it holds within itself for its future. During this stage of profound transformation, imaginal cells appear, cluster, and then start to form the beginning of a new reality. This is an evolutionary leap, and a new reality is being birthed that eventually leads to a new form: a butterfly. The caterpillar cannot become a butterfly unless and until it goes through the chaos and mess of transformation.

Maybe this is true for us as well. The mess and chaos of the step-learn-experiment approach, and the mess and chaos of the obstacles we experience along the way, are a profound opportunity, and maybe even a necessity, for our transformation and lasting change.

Success, in my mind, is related to how powerfully we can make an impact on what matters most to each of us regardless of our profession, our politics, or our personal circumstances.

Now you are ready to put everything you have learned together as you continue moving your next bold move forward. Chapter 9 is about helping you stay focused on how to move forward so that it serves you best. The way you move forward must fit you specifically as you learn how to be flexible to what works best for you.

Stay tuned for Chapter 9, *Dance and Weave*.

Additional Resources

Here is a list of things that I read, listen to, or watch to help me *Generate Some STEAM*.

Books:

Execution: The Discipline of Getting Things Done by Larry Bossidy and Ram Charan

The 7 Habits of Highly Successful People by Stephen R. Covey

Just Start: Take Action, Embrace Uncertainty, Create the Future by Leonard A. Schlesinger and Charles F. Kiefer

Videos:

John Goddard: Adventurer, Explorer, and Goal Achiever
http://www.youtube.com/watch?v=Zy95I0Mb16E

Jon Kabat-Zinn on Awareness and Mindfulness
http://www.youtube.com/watch?v=3nwwKbM_vJc

Websites:

Prendismo
Over 15,000 two-minute clips on entrepreneurship, business, and leadership.
www.prendismo.com/collection/

Entrepreneur
News, advice, and strategy for businesses.
www.entrepreneur.com

State of Grace Document
The blueprint of We. Build and sustain healthier business and personal relationships.
www.stateofgracedocument.com

Music:

"For the Love of Money" by The O'Jays

"Pump It" by the Black Eyed Peas

"Stand and Be Counted" by Crosby, Stills, Nash & Young

Chapter 9

Dance and Weave

This chapter is a synthesis of the **9 Steps** as you continue to move toward and celebrate your next bold move. Now is the time for you to step fully into the game, step up into your power, and dance with the love of creating what's next for yourself with something you really, really want. Following these steps as you create your next bold move in the world is like weaving together the steps in the way that serves you best, moving toward your future self like a strand of silk woven into a beautiful quilt. Integrate all that you learn along the way and celebrate yourself. Dance and weave. As William Purkey says, "You've gotta dance like there's nobody watching." The point is to move through the **9 Steps** and enjoy the ride, and remember to lighten up so you have some fun along the way.

Writing this book has been a bold move for me. I don't see myself as a writer. When I first imagined myself as an author, I either laughed or rolled my eyes at the absurdity of the idea. And yet, each time I listened up to my intuition during my time-outs, my masculine side kept going back to the idea and thinking about what it might look like, how I might find the time to write, the actual process of writing and having someone else edit each chapter, etc. My masculine, logical side was figuring out the how-tos. My feminine side, that internal quiet voice of mine I have come to adore and trust, just kept repeating over and over again, "Just write darling. We'll take care of the rest. There is nothing else for you to do right now, just write."

Combining both my masculine and my feminine skills and blending them together meant I miraculously wrote my entire first draft in just four weeks. My masculine linear and logical side created the outline, the two-hour block I would use to write each day, the thought process to put thoughts to paper, and the smarts to discipline myself to be alone while I wrote. My feminine, creative, nonjudgmental side helped the words fly onto my computer screen, and helped me soothe myself when I got stuck as I heard my internal voice say, "It's okay, don't worry, you are meant to write this. Keep going." If I had thought about it and how writing used to be so hard for me and how I wouldn't ever really find the time, interest, and energy to write, I would not have completed the project. With a little dance and weave of the masculine and the feminine, somehow this book got written.

As part of your next bold move, continue to practice weaving the masculine and feminine approaches and styles into your own life. Sometimes it is easy. Sometimes it is not. Notice when you are overusing one or the other style and make a conscious effort to enhance your current situation by adding the less-used approach to your routine. When I was over-analyzing whether I should carve out the time to work on this book, I called upon my feminine style to help me sort out the situation. And I remembered to connect to what's most important to me, which is helping other people sparkle through the use of their gifts and talents, one bold move at a time.

Remember to love and embrace the linear masculine side that allows you to use your power, drive, and mastery to obtain those things that can be controlled. Your warrior side. The rational, objective, driven-toward-results, achievement-oriented, and competitive side, where these attributes all align to get you what you want. Power and results. Action and accomplishment. That's you in all your masculine glory!

Remember to love and embrace your creative, intuitive feminine side and use it to co-create with others those things beyond your reach for which your heart most deeply longs. This is the side of you that doesn't know the answers or even how you will get there, but knows somewhere deep inside that you want it and must have it, nonetheless. The side of you that loves deeply, cares and wants to contribute to the world, collaborates, is values-centric, cultivates mutually respectful relationships, and that is unwaveringly positioned true north toward your purpose and passions. Ask yourself over and over again, what is calling you forward? And listen, always quiet, contemplative, aligning who you are and what you do with what has the most meaning for you and with your purpose. Then with a deep inner knowing, call on your intuition to advise you as you make your next move. That's you in all your feminine glory!

Getting Started

Weave together the masculine and the feminine with your mind and your heart, using your intuition and your drive to get anything and everything you have ever wanted. The extraordinary ways of the masculine and the feminine coming together helps us create and then execute, weaving together a beautiful tapestry of your heart's desire that will enrich your life and the lives of those you touch. Maybe you will even leave a legacy. Maybe you will make a contribution beyond your wildest dreams. Maybe, just maybe, your next bold move will shape your life anew in ways you cannot even begin to imagine. Allow yourself to enjoy the mystery as it unfolds over time.

I sometimes wonder, What if I do not have all the answers? And, of course, I don't. But what if I relaxed the side of me that wants to know exactly what to do and exactly what will happen if I do it, and exactly what to expect at all times? Would I be as happy, or is the mystery that unfolds as we all dance and weave and practice stepping, one step at a time, the most delicious part? I wonder.

We as Americans tend to jump too quickly into action. We are so hungry for results, as our masculine style likes to manage by objective and create urgent deadlines to meet. What if creating your next bold move allowed you to see the mystery, the treasure hunt that the Universe has planned for you? What if you really could follow your dreams by following the *9 Steps to Your Next Bold Move*? What if it just required nine simple steps taken one at a time, methodically, checking off one step at a time like the masculine would approach it, or moving back and forth between the steps to bring forth a rhythm that works for you best, like the feminine approach. What if? I wonder.

My dear friend Martha Freyman Miser wrote in her Ph.D. dissertation, *The Myth of Endless Accumulation: A Feminist Inquiry into Globalization, Growth, and Social Change*, "What is the future I want from the world around me, and how do my actions align with that future?"

What is the future you want, my dear girlfriend? And what will you do and who will you be as you decide to go after it? Although I don't know who said it, I love the saying, "Who you *be* speaks louder than what you *do*." Weaving together the masculine and the feminine has us weave being in action with just *being*, making both of these important in creating our next step. I wonder what you will discover as you swim around in the delicious energy and path toward your next bold move.

Exercises and Activities

Answer the questions below to help you execute more successfully.

• Track your progress toward your next bold move by writing down three accomplishments you are proud of from the last three months.

- Honor your feminine style by putting a quiet, creative practice into your life daily. You know you are headed in the right direction if you find your mind wandering aimlessly (this is a good thing!).

Brainstormers to Dance and Weave

1. If we had all the answers, life would not be so rich and interesting. The mystery, as risky as it is sometimes, is the very thing that excites us and adds more color to our lives.
2. Expect the unexpected and enjoy. Learn to let go.
3. Create a structure that allows you to know what to do and when to do it. Then analyze what's working and what isn't.
4. Have concise goals, a clear statement of success with outcomes you desire, and a methodology to get there. Continue to work your plan until you get to where you want to go.

Summary

Use all that you have learned from the previous chapters like a toolbox as you dance and weave between the steps; taking out the right tool from your box to use depending on where you are in your process and journey. Sometimes you might be more quiet as you need the tool of more inner guidance, as you 'Check Your Inner State', 'Take a Time-Out', and 'Listen UP! to Your Intuition'. Another time you might need more support as you Surround Yourself With Extreme Support' or 'Gather in Purposeful Community'. Other times you might need your action tool as you, 'Prepare for the Game', 'Get Clear About What You Want', and 'Make Some STEAM'.

Additional Resources

Here is a list of things that I read, listen to, or watch to help me *Dance and Weave.*

Books:

The Big Leap: Conquer Your Hidden Fear and Take Your Life to the Next Level
by Gay Hendricks

A New Earth: Awakening to Your Life's Purpose by Eckhart Tolle

Power Vs. Force: The Hidden Determinants of Human Behavior by David R. Hawkins

Videos:

Judson Laipply: Evolution of Dance 2
http://www.youtube.com/watch?v=inLBPVG8oEU

Where the Hell is Matt?
http://www.youtube.com/watch?v=zlfKdbWwruY

Music:

"**Life is a Highway**" by Tom Cochrane

"**Simply the Best**" by Tina Turner

"**I Believe I Can Fly**" by R. Kelly

"**I'm About to Come Alive**" by Train

Chapter 10

Moving Yourself Forward

Use this book over and over again to help you make each bold move. Let this text serve as your template and as part of your support to keep you in check and remind you to take the next step. As you make a bold move, remember to rest and celebrate before jumping too fast into the next one. Rest. Replenish. Have a cup of tea with a girlfriend. And then check in with your inner guidance to see where to head next.

Remind yourself that this journey of yours requires quiet and the courage to look at what you want, and to make it happen. You cannot do it alone. You are not meant to do it alone. Girlfriend helping girlfriend and the holding, nurturing, and witnessing of community. Your community of support. And it's just one step at a time, **9** of them to be precise, to create a life you fall in love with.

More Additional Resources

If you want more resources to develop yourself as a leader and to join a community of women who are already helping each other make their dreams come true and accomplishing their next bold moves, here you go:

Corporate Women's Leadership: Programs and workshops for organizations to bring in-house for their women's leadership development initiatives. We provide leading edge workshops, keynotes, lunch and learns to develop, retain and inspire corporate leadership talent for women and sometimes even include the men who work with them.
http://visionquestconsulting.com/womens-leadership/

Women's Personal Leadership Retreats: Women supporting women to make their next bold move through our special brand of community and collaboration. Retreats for women who want to develop their leadership, re-shape their future, and be part of a network of supportive like-minded women.
http://visionquestconsulting.com/events/

Vision to Success Workshop: A one-day workshop for individuals (men and women) interested in moving a professional (business, career or entrepreneurial) venture forward. Participants leave this workshop with a strategic action planning guide to move themselves forward. You'll be amazed at how much progress you can make in with our unique, step-by-step approach.
http://visionquestconsulting.com/vision-to-success/

The Women's Summer Retreat: A once a year opportunity and retreat for women who want to turn a life or career goal into reality. The Women's Summer Retreat is a unique blend of personal and professional leadership development with a focus on personal growth and transformation in the context of community.
http://visionquestconsulting.com/womens-summer-retreat/

Next Bold Move Television Broadcast: Our TV show on leadership and personal development to help individuals move their next bold move forward.
http://visionquestconsulting.com/your-next-bold-move-broadcasts/
and
http://www.youtube.com/channel/UCpLOhaOEzKB2UmMiLh-cvCw

About the Author

Wendy Capland, author of *"Your Next Bold Move for Women; 9 Proven Steps to Everything You Ever Wanted"* is CEO of <u>Vision Quest Consulting</u>, a management consulting firm founded in 1987, specializing in developing individual and organizational leadership talent.

Professionally, Wendy is one of the top female leaders in America and has worked with thousands of individuals helping them expand their leadership capabilities and reach their professional goals. Her professional accolades include:

- Over 20 years of experience working with Fortune 500 companies, start ups, and individual entrepreneurs to help them increase their impact and results and who go forth to make a bigger bolder difference in their organizations and in the world
- Pioneer in the field of Executive Coaching and Leadership Development in organizations
- Past-President and Board member of the International Coach Federation-New England
- Producer of *Your Next Bold Move* television series, broadcasted in over 2.5 million households monthly for over 3 years
- Executive Coaching partner with Simmons Leadership Conference, providing workshops and Executive Coaching for over 3000 attendees

Personally, Wendy has dedicated her life to helping others discover their greatness, their gifts and talents, and who they are meant to "be" in the world as they make their personal and professional lives a dream come true. She is an avid skier, plays a mean game of ping-pong, and is a lifelong learner in the arena of balancing the health of her body, mind, and spirit.

Wendy lives in Massachusetts with her husband and family.

Acknowledgements

One day, while I was teaching a workshop on courage, a woman raised her hand and asked me if I had thought about writing a book about the things I was teaching. "No, I'm not a writer," I replied quickly. And then I started to wonder if I could be. Her question nagged at me for about a year until I finally thought, "Why not, maybe my tried-and-true steps to create something bold could help others." And so my journey toward becoming an author began, and **Your Next Bold Move** was born.

My first and biggest thank you to my husband, Chris, who, while on our summer vacation, left the house every morning for a few hours so that I could write uninterrupted. And more importantly, for the endless love he has for me. I am so thankful for the life we have created together, which I hardly dreamed could be possible.

To my wonderful children, siblings, and parents, who endlessly support and love me, which provides a solid foundation for all of who I am, and all of who I have yet to become. A special thank you to my mother, who has told me since the day I was born that I was born under a lucky star. And to my dad, who since I was 12 years old, instilled in me the belief that anything was possible if I really wanted it.

To my dear friend Mary Elizabeth Wheeler, who edited this manuscript with loving care and masterful technical ability.

To Ann Crews Melton, who proofread the final copy with an eagle eye and expert attention to detail.

And to my magical girlfriends, who have been my lifeline and sisters of my heart: Mel, Donna, Kate, Kelly, Wynne, Cindy, and Sue. I would never have written this without you!

Made in the USA
Charleston, SC
15 February 2016